Amos Kidder Fiske

Beyond the bourn

Reports of a traveller returned

Amos Kidder Fiske
Beyond the bourn
Reports of a traveller returned
ISBN/EAN: 9783337209957

Printed in Europe, USA, Canada, Australia, Japan

Cover: Foto ©Andreas Hilbeck / pixelio.de

More available books at **www.hansebooks.com**

BEYOND THE BOURN

Reports

OF A TRAVELLER RETURNED FROM
"THE UNDISCOVERED COUNTRY"

SUBMITTED TO THE WORLD BY

AMOS K. FISKE

Author of "Midnight Talks at The Club"

NEW YORK
FORDS, HOWARD, & HULBERT
1891

Copyright in 1891
By AMOS K. FISKE

PREFATORY NOTE.

THE manuscript, from which the bulk of this volume is made up, came into the hands of the present editor nearly eighteen years ago. He was doubtful, then, whether the world was ready to give heed to the revelation which it purported to contain. He is not certain yet. During that long period this strange account of a disembodied experience has been submitted in confidence to more than one competent judge of the expediency of publication, but not until recently had the response been encouraging. At last the editor feels justified in discharging himself of the responsibility implied in the acceptance of a manuscript intrusted to him in the evident expectation that sooner or later he would give it to the world.

If it contains any message to mankind of which mankind feels the need, it will doubtless be listened to. If not, it may be allowed to pass unheeded, like those weird utterances, which the dazed mind fails to grasp, of

"Airy tongues that syllable men's names
  On sands, and shores and desert wildernesses."

AMOS K. FISKE.

NEW YORK, March, 1891.

CONTENTS.

                                                                              PAGE

I.
THE STRANGER AND HIS MANUSCRIPT, . . 1

II.
A TALE OF LIFE AND DEATH, ... 11

III.
IN THE OTHER WORLD, ... 30

IV.
"THE LIFE INDEED," 47

V.
THE SECRET OF GROWTH, ... 58

VI.
DISCOURSE OF A HEAVENLY SAGE, . . . 67

VII.
LIFE ON A DISTANT SPHERE, . . . 81

CONTENTS.

PAGE

VIII.
PROGRESS OF A PERFECT RACE, . . . 103

IX.
THE HIGHER MORALS AND RELIGION, . . 121

X.
SPIRIT RELATIONSHIP AND ACHIEVEMENT, . 147

XI.
SNATCHED FROM THE HEAVENLY LIFE, . . 172

XII.
MAN'S REVELATION TO MAN, . . . 184

BEYOND THE BOURN

I.

THE STRANGER AND HIS MANUSCRIPT.

It was in the summer of 1873 that I took my wife and infant child and left the great, hot city of New York to find refreshment for body and mind in a quiet retreat in the country. We did not go to watering place or popular resort, but sought out a little inland nook not far from the Hudson River, where we were completely shut off from all hint of the busy metropolis and the cares and labors that we had left behind, and gave ourselves up to a four weeks' revel in the joys of the green summer time.

The place was a bit of a farm, on a brown and dusty road which slipped away from the great highways of steamboat and locomotive into a secluded valley, a patchwork of pasture, field and woodland, kept always green by one garrulous stream and many rills which fed it from the mists on the mountains. I had known the house and its mistress from boyhood, and found there what I wanted, simple fare and complete freedom. There were two or three others of kindred tastes who passed some summer weeks at the place and gave the good woman, in return for healthful hospitality, a little surplus of money to carry her through the winter.

Among these visitors in that particular summer was one I had not seen before. We found him there when we came, but received no introduction, and he kept himself a stranger in the little hostelry. He was the most mysterious human being I ever met: tall and well formed, with a face that was hardly handsome, but had a fascinating quality that led one to look at him often and long. He bore himself as one having no part with company into which he was thrown. His dark hair fell carelessly over a white brow, and his eyes had a far-away look which showed that his thoughts were seldom with his body or its surroundings. He appeared hardly conscious that he was an object of attention, and if spoken to, which rarely happened, seemed to be recalled from a revery which he would rather had not been disturbed. On the side of his neck and forehead were some large scars in which a slight inflammation furnished almost the only flush of color about his countenance. When forced to speak, it was in a low, quiet tone, with the least touch of impatience at being drawn from his communion with the far-off world in which he seemed to live. He seldom smiled, and then in a pensive way that provoked no responsive smile, but had rather a depressing effect. Once or twice I tried to call him out with a question or a statement about the affairs of the world beyond our little retreat. He listened respectfully, but with no sign of interest in the subject, and in his answers gave evidence that these matters never occupied his thoughts.

For my own part I love social converse, and, when withdrawn from the busy world and its exciting topics of news and of thought, am fond of talks on various themes, the wonders of nature about us, the great and manifold mysteries of the heavens over our heads, the thousand relations and obligations of the family of mankind in this life, and their probable destiny and relations hereafter. The mind will be busy; and, when shut out from commerce, from politics, from all bustling affairs that distract it in our working weeks, what more wholesome subjects than these, for which we have little time save in the summer holiday? Then we can return to unwritten philosophy and poetry, which were wont to carry our dreaming youth above and beyond the world on wings of speculation.

I could not forego my summer talk on

these things,—my little disputations and discussions with our circle at table or around the evening porch, notwithstanding the somewhat chilling presence of the mysterious guest. Occasionally, when I queried about the mysteries of the unseen world, the life of the departed and the life to come to us all, he showed an interest in the conversation and would seem to be listening. As he glanced up now and then, the peculiar look of his eyes —the habitual air of remoteness, as if the soul had left looking from her windows and was musing on invisible scenes— would disappear, and he seemed for the time to draw into our circle, though he spoke no word and made no response to what others said. The look of interest sometimes deepened to one almost of pity, as if there were things in his thoughts far deeper, higher and truer than those he heard, but things so unutterable that it was useless to try to speak them.

I began at last to regard this as

the heart of his mystery. Some great experience, I thought, or a nature of unusual spirituality and strange insight into things unseen by others, has given him a cast of thought out of sympathy with our common life. His thoughts are not the thoughts of other men, and they are of a kind to make him silent and lonely among his fellows.

Of the man's life I could learn nothing. In all his habits he was quiet and seclusive, and his reticence was of a kind that compelled respect. No one liked to question him. He had been attracted by the cottage and its romantic surroundings in passing, early in the season, and asked permission to spend the summer there at whatever rate of compensation was right. He wished to be known as Mr. Jameson, merely, would give little trouble, and preferred to be left altogether to himself. His history like his character was a mystery, and none of us could penetrate it.

The time drew near when we must give

up our paradisian holiday and go back to the cares and business of the world. Our good landlady told us that on the day previous to our intended departure Mr. Jameson was going, but she knew not whither. On the evening before he was to go, I had wandered down the road, as I often did, and stood gazing into the deep and quiet heavens, while the drowsy babble of the brook and the faint whisper of the wind in the shrubbery mingled in my ears, and carried my soul off into dreamy speculations. Suddenly I was recalled from my revery by a touch on the arm, and found our strange friend, for so he had become in spite of his unsocial reticence, standing by me.

"I go away to-morrow," he said, "and you, soon after. I know what you all think of me. I am a mystery to you and to all that see me, but I cannot help it. I live within myself because I can live in no other way. I have had an experience which perhaps ought to be made known, but I cannot tell it in my own person. I I have found in you one nearer in sympathy with me than any I ever expected to meet in this world, and to you I have determined to intrust a crude record of this experience, which you may make known or not, as may seem to you best."

With this, he handed me a roll of manuscript, and became as silent as ever, as we walked quietly back to the cottage. When I rose in the morning he was gone. All his arrangements had been made on the previous evening and no one knew when or how he went. I examined the roll of manuscript and found it contained a narrative which the author had entitled,

"A New Revelation."

Since then the MS. has lain most of the time undisturbed in a drawer with other papers, though several times I have taken it out and gone over the strange tale, doubting whether the public would take an interest in it, or whether the time were ripe for the sort of "revelation" which it offered. Finally I have concluded that the only way to test these questions is to give the story to the world; indeed I have felt under a sort of implied obligation to do so sooner or later, in accepting it from the hands of its author. If he has continued in the land of the living—a point upon which I have never been able to obtain any light since that summer evening long past—he must have concluded that I did not consider it worth while to publish his "revelation." Perhaps he may have assumed that I had doubts of its genuineness and good faith; but if so, he has never taken the trouble to reassure me on that point. I make no question at all of the reality of the experience narrated; but as I have found it interesting to myself, and consider the speculations that are involved with it very suggestive, to say the least, I venture at last to have it put in print.

And I do this, whether the great public, with its manifold occupations and diversions, shall give it the attention which its lofty themes ought to command, or whether it shall permit the long buried MS. to sink into permanent obscurity.

II.

A TALE OF LIFE AND DEATH.

A FEW years ago I was one of the happiest of men, in my domestic relations. My father, who was old while I was still quite young, had accumulated during a long and industrious life a goodly competence, and we lived modestly but most comfortably in our home by one of the lovely lakes in the interior of New York State. I was always sensitive and shy, and my acquaintance beyond our own little circle was slight. The best of my education was obtained at a High School near by, but books, pictures and music always gave a degree of unpretentious refinement to our home and were a source of constant pleasure to me. I had a sister two years younger than myself, tender and affectionate, with a fragile constitution which was calculated to awaken solicitude while it deepened attachment. We were the only children of the family, and to our welfare our kindly parents were entirely devoted, treating all our wishes with as much indulgence as was consistent with wisdom. The result was an unusually devoted affection between the members of the family.

Love for my gentle sister would probably have been still more absorbing with me, as we grew up together, but for a division of sentiment which favoring circumstances brought about for both of us. A boy of the neighborhood came to be my companion at an early age, and we were so constituted in our differences of taste and temperament as to produce one of those strong and romantic friendships which have been the subjects of story in all ages. Robert Ellis had an ardent and robust nature, full of ambition and enthusiasm, but with an honesty and candor that gave it the simplicity of untarnished childhood so long as I knew him; while I was timid and shrinking, so far as the contests of life affected me at all. Perhaps it was his strength and courage and eagerness for the strife, that excited my special admiration and gained my devoted affection; while he may have been won to me by a gentleness and dependence that touched the heroic in his nature. At any rate as boys we were "all in all" to each other; and as we came to manhood only his sister and mine divided the treasure of our affections. His sister Lucy was the feminine counterpart of himself, full of the ardor and eagerness of young life, hopeful and cheery, and as truthful and free from guile as Nature herself. I do not profess to understand the psychology of those two affections, but the absorbing love which I came to have for his sister, made perfect by a full return from her own ardent nature, in no way impaired my strong friendship for the brother. In the meantime my own fragile sister had somehow grown into his manly heart with a hold as strong as life. Here was a quartet of human souls, knit together by the interlacing bonds of mutual affection, which it would be death to sunder.

Until the age of twenty-five, my life had been without a shadow, and promised a future as serene and happy; but it is rare that Heaven vouchsafes to man a life of uninterrupted felicity. Each must take his share of trouble and sorrow, and if it comes late and he has had no foretaste, it will be so much the harder to bear. The great but ever-merciful Power that holds us in his keeping, seems to have chosen me for affliction, perhaps that out of it might come some great good.

The first cloud to come across my serene sky was the death of my father and mother, which occurred in the same week; but they had become old, and their departure was not unlooked for. Moreover, they had seen me happily married, and were ready to leave me master of the homestead and father of a family to come. Yes, I was happily married to one whose heart had never been touched by thought of love for any other in the same kind, but was mine wholly, and one whose dominion over my soul was complete and undisputed—the sister of my dearest friend.

The loss of our parents would have been much harder for my gentle sister, Ellen, but for the fact that she was already affianced to Robert Ellis, and had his strong nature to rest upon, as well as all the support to be derived from the devoted affection of myself and my wife. She had a home with us, and a happy home of her own in view, and it was but natural that even her sensitive nature should bear this first sorrow with some degree of composure. For myself it was not hard. It gave to my quiet moments a deeper thoughtfulness, and to the dusk of evening at times a solemn sadness, as if sanctified by the presence of the departed ones. They had passed on without regret, and awaited us in a home which we confidently expected to share when our call should come.

But at no great interval after this first sorrow came a succession of pitiless blows of affliction. The terrible war of 1861 had come upon the country, with its volume of tragedies for American homes. My friend was by nature a patriot and a hero, and he could not resist the call to what he deemed the post of duty for every man who was free to go to the defence of the Union and of the cause of liberty. Even his love for my sister, whom he expected soon to take under his care for life, could not overcome in his mind that profound sense of obligation to take his part in saving the life of the nation. He pleaded that it would only postpone their happiness, and that it would make him more worthy of it; in fact, he should always feel like a craven if he did not make this brief sacrifice for a cause more sacred than any private claim. The poor girl sympathized fully with his feeling, and, though with many tears and secret misgivings, she encouraged him to go. She would follow him with her heart, and await his return with hope of increased joy.

The pitiful parting took place, and our hero departed for the field of danger, followed with foreboding, on my part at least. Aside from the perils of the great conflict and the uncertain fate to which he committed himself, his absence was in itself a bereavement to our home. I confess that I had not the heroic temper that would induce me to accompany him in any case. I was fond of quiet and retirement and little given to energetic action, and neither the duties nor the hardships of war had any attraction for me. But plainly I had excuse enough in the care of those now left to my exclusive charge, and no human power could have torn me from my wife and home, the idol of my worship and its temple.

The adventures of the camp and of the battle-field, the vicissitudes of a soldier's life, came to us in an ever-continued story from our patriot friend, told with unflagging spirit and never wavering cheerfulness and hope. It was pathetic to see how completely my poor sister's life and thoughts were absorbed in this intermittent tale of real life, of which the outcome was shrouded in more thrilling uncertainty than novelist could devise for his fiction, and it was plainly evident that a fatal catastrophe to the hero would snap her own frail hold upon life.

Suddenly, in the dark days of '63 the tale of his adventures was broken short; to be continued to an abrupt close by "another hand." After a period of anxious waiting the dreaded word from the new and unknown writer came. Our beloved friend had been struck down in the midst of battle in the cornfields of Gettysburg. Death was immediate, without preliminary suffering, without last words or loving message, save such as had been sealed up in anticipation of possible fatality on the field. My sister received the news with tearless pallor, and it seemed as though she had been expecting it all these two heavy years. She uttered no word or wail of sorrow, she fell under no sudden stroke of prostration, but she clung to life under the strain of the days that intervened before the mangled body of her heroic lover came to deepen the gloom of our home.

Fortunately, the noble face and head were not marred, and on the calm lineaments rested the promise of immortal peace. In the silent and darkened room in which the casket was placed, with only the face of the dead uncovered, we left Ellen alone, according to her wish. When at last we quietly went in, intending with all gentleness to draw her away, her arms were encircling the head and her face resting upon the face of the husband of her heart, and she too was dead, with a smile upon her lips. Perhaps the two souls had met there and departed together to fulfil the promises made on earth.

We buried them side by side in the

beautiful cemetery by the lake, and with aching hearts heaped flowers on the double grave, striving so far as possible to drive away the gloom of death.

Now only wife and home were left to me this side the shadows, and oh! how I clung to them,—almost with fear and trembling lest they should go too. And it seems the pitying heavens must needs have them, for a few months later my darling was torn from me, in the struggle to bring a new soul from God to dwell in our home and perchance to give us comfort for the losses of the past. But she perished in a mission too severe for her vitality, which had been impaired by recent afflictions; and the new soul, too, fluttered for a moment on the verge of earthly life and went back to God. There was another burial; and father, mother, sister, friend, wife and babe, lay side by side in the green churchyard by the placid lake.

Then the home that had been so bright and beautiful was utterly desolate. It seemed as though some unmerciful spirit had come in at that door again and again, and carried away amid funeral odors and a thickening gloom each time a more precious treasure, till nothing was left. My loneliness and misery were unutterable in the home now so completely bereft. To seek oblivion in narcotics or stimulants was a repulsive folly, and there was no hope that forgetfulness would come of itself. My mind was too strong to break down and find relief in disorganization and mental chaos. My occupations at home instead of taking my thoughts from my losses continually recalled them to me.

I determined to sell my homestead and seek in the great world, of which I knew so little, that distraction which alone could save me from settled melancholy and utter wretchedness. This I did. A part of the proceeds of the sale were invested to form a fund for future resource; the rest converted into cash for immediate use. I then set out on my travels.

I visited the cities of the Atlantic coast in my own country, and went to the great prairies and lakes, to the mountains and the backwoods. I crossed the rocky ridges to the Pacific side and sought out the wonders of that marvellous region. Returning I went to Europe and visited her capitals, and extended my wandering among the mystic monuments of Egypt and Arabia, and the sacred reminiscences of Palestine.

Everywhere I sought for whatever could interest and absorb the thoughts. The constant succession of new things, the continual occupation of the mind with the wonders of the earth, overwhelmed the old grief and wrought through meditation a philosophy which imparted some degree of calm resignation, though the joy of youthful life was gone out forever. I returned from these wanderings after five years, older by a century in experience,—philosophic and thoughtful, and if not quite happy, at least not altogether wretched.

On returning from over the sea I landed in Canada, as I had not visited that country before leaving my native land. I went up the St. Lawrence and viewed what has most semblance of the ancient in our Northern-Western continent; and then—with emotions that no man could describe or fully conceive unless he had been through a like experience—I entered my native land once more, and set out to pass through the length of Vermont towards the older cities of the Atlantic coast. There I proposed to spend the rest of my days amid books and the converse of such men as my travelled lore might bring me acquainted with.

It was late in the spring and I was riding on a railroad train through a wild and rugged part of the Green Mountain state. Late in the afternoon heavy black clouds rolled into the heavens from beyond the ridges to the west, and ominous rumblings of thunder uttered threats of a storm of uncommon violence. The train rattled on as the darkness thickened, and shortly after sunset we were plunging madly through a black gloom, occasionally filled with a lurid light as the flashes of lightning sprang into it and disappeared again. Presently the rain came in torrents and the wind dashed it against the cars as if determined to throw them from the track. Still the engineer dashed on, hauling us through the storm at what seemed a frightful speed. Crashes of thunder came as if the heavens were breaking in pieces, and we almost expected that the fierce flashes that followed would show us the fragments of the collapsing universe. But each time nature sprang into being as from a new chaos; for a moment trees struggling with the tempest, rocks and gorges over which the accumulating waters dashed wildly as if in fright, appeared and were again swallowed by the darkness. The noise of the wheels and shrieks of the engine mingling with the tremendous hurlyburly of the elements was appalling.

In the car, dimly lighted with two or

three wretched lamps, the passengers sat oppressed with a vague fear, as if waiting for some inevitable crash, the consequences of which they could not guess. Once or twice the car gave an ugly lurch and plunge, and the engineer slackened somewhat his terrific speed. This caution seemed to frighten us even more than the previous recklessness, as it indicated real danger. By and by came a plunge which threw everybody out of his seat, then a succession of heavy thumps which threatened to disjoint the frame, and the carriage was left pitched into the mud, while those behind dashed upon it and the engine sped off down the track.

Everybody was bruised and terribly frightened, but no one was badly hurt. A culvert had been washed away by the torrent and the track had sunk from its proper level. The engine and baggage car had passed safely over, but the car in which I sat was thrown from the track and its coupling broken. The train had been brought to a very slow speed, and hence our escape from destruction. It was fortunate that few passengers travelled on the night train, for we were still in the wilderness, far from any comfortable accommodations.

The conductor came around, swinging his lantern in the darkness and glistening in his india-rubber coat, and got us all together, wet and shivering and battered by the pitiless storm. The engine backed up, and stood glaring and snorting as if the wild scene and the fierce weather just suited its temper. In fact it looked like a horrible monster, waiting impatiently for us to put ourselves in his power once more, and determined that we should not escape so easily again. It appeared that it was impracticable to repair the track and get the cars into position to proceed, and we must needs crowd into the baggage car to be taken to the next station. It seemed like a perilous experiment, but there was no choice except to stay there in the darkness and rain, in what to us was an unknown wilderness. The conductor said there was no danger, but each man felt that he knew better and went into the dismal baggage car with a shudder and a silent protest. It was a rough affair, half filled with trunks and boxes and lighted by two sickly lanterns.

We bestowed ourselves as best we could, crowded together like cattle, drenched with rain, and in anything but a cheerful mood. The engineer started on, and soon we seemed to be plunging down a grade at a furious speed. Perhaps our fears and our uncomfortable position exaggerated to our minds the rate at which we were going but it seemed tremendous, and faces grew pale and eyes gleamed with excitement in the darkness. Some one remonstrated with the conductor. The engine had little to draw and was evidently on a descending grade. The torrents from the hills were likely to undermine the track at any point. The danger was evident, and it was sheer recklessness to proceed except with the greatest caution. The conductor had just seized the cord to give the signal to the engineer to slacken his speed when one terrific crash came, followed by a shock that seemed to wrench my body to pieces, and the car and all its contents were dashed in fragments upon the glowing, raving engine, which was thrown over and screeching as if with horror at its own work.

I was conscious of being crushed and immovable in a mass of fragments; I knew that I was fearfully cut and bruised about the head and neck; I heard groans and shrieks of such mingled pain and horror that they almost made me forget my own situation. Soon the crushing weight and the fierce pain became insupportable, and, to add to the horrors of the situation, scalding steam and burning heat from the engine fire were at once boiling and roasting us.

As I realized after the first quick consciousness of what had happened, that I was utterly helpless, probably fatally hurt, and almost sure to be burned or scalded to death on the spot, a strange and awful feeling came over me. Here was death suddenly upon me, which I had regarded only as a vague and far off fate. In a moment I should be in the other world and all its mystery. My past life, its early happiness, the shock of its great sorrows, the slow and painful healing of the wounds in these later years,— all occurred to me in a moment, and I thought of the doubts that I sometimes felt, of the immortality of the soul and of the happiness or misery of a future life. I rejoiced that I had little to reproach myself with beyond the small failings for which poor human nature can readily find excuse, and that I could meet whatever was now to come without faltering. One moment of fierce agony, a shock that wrenched my whole body as if by the sundering of the flesh and spirit, and I seemed to sink and glide immeasurable lengths and depths at a dizzy speed into darkness and oblivion.

III.

IN THE OTHER WORLD.

AFTER a stretch of time which I could not measure, which might have been moments and might have been ages, I was conscious of renewed existence and of the presence of other beings. As that consciousness grew clear, intense, almost overwhelming in its fulness, I knew that I was in the spirit world and with the beloved of former years.

The nature of that consciousness I cannot hope to describe in the language of earth, or make clear to minds that never experienced it. I had no body; and yet felt my identity, my personal presence, with a completeness and intensity that was altogether new. I saw not and heard not, in the earthly sense; and yet my knowledge of my surroundings and of the presence of others was far more distinct than bodily sight and hearing could make it. We spake not with tongues of flesh, we heard not with ears of flesh, and yet our communication was so perfect that I marvelled as at a new birth. The soul was freed from the impediment of flesh, it acted without the cumbersome instrumentality of physical organs, and its action was full and free.

It will be difficult to make the conditions of my new life comprehensible to those whose experience has been confined to the embryonic stage of human existence, but the faculties of the soul were not changed, and its perceptions were analogous to those to which it had been accustomed. It had no further need of physical senses, and yet it saw and heard and felt with a clearness and vividness that were unattainable through the organs of the body. It could enjoy now the full benefit of the development which it had attained with the aid of the body and its functions, and exercise its faculties with a freedom and vigor that were impossible when it was confined in the integument of flesh.

In attempting to put into the form of human speech a description of the surroundings in which I found myself, and an account of the experience which I underwent, it will be possible to give only a faint impression of the reality, for the language of man is inadequate to express and the understanding of man incapable of grasping the facts of an experience and observation beyond the range of earthly life. The effort to picture it is like striving to reveal the beauties of a glorious vision through an imperfect medium to a darkened mind; but it may afford glimpses that will give comfort to those who long to know something of the life beyond.

First of all I would try to give some idea of the recompense that was found for the trials, struggles and sorrows of the earthly life. These seemed as small and far away in comparison with the satisfaction now enjoyed, as the sphere on which they were undergone seemed insignificant, as a part of God's creation. Here I found father and mother in a blissful union that was marred by no discordant note and no fear of interruption. They looked back to their former life with thankfulness that it had prepared them for this, but they would no more desire to return to it than a miner who had toiled for years in the bowels of the earth would wish to go back to his wearisome tasks, if once released and placed in comfortable and joyous surroundings in the cheerful sunlight. To them had now been gathered the children they left behind, and the mutual understanding and full appreciation of each other gave their communion a delight that was before inconceivable.

The coming of their daughter, which to me had been such a grief, was to them and to her a joy unspeakable. In the body she had been frail and an object of solicitude, but in the spirit world she blossomed to the fulness of angelic life at once. The attributes that had been cramped by physical weakness and narrow opportunities expanded in their full glory, and that pure love which had been awakened on earth found a purer fruition because it had never been sullied by the harsh experiences of a common life. She had been literally carried to heaven by her hero lover, who lingered, " hovering o'er the dolorous strait," that they might together " arrive at last the blessed goal " and be taken " as a single soul." So had they been united in the marriage of eternity by death itself,—in a union that no trial or sorrow could ever assail, for which only the pure in heart are fit. My own beloved wife, and the babe that had known nothing of the earthly life, which had opened and shut for it merely as a gateway to heaven—during my sorrowful wanderings they had awaited me with happiness unalloyed, knowing how great would be the joy of reunion, and how small would then seem the delay and the sorrows I had borne, which would only heighten the bliss. And the little one had grown in this life like one native to it, developing in spiritual purity and strength with scarcely a taint of earth. Here was a happy family, in a sense that no combination of fortunate circumstances could make real in the conditions of earth, associated with other families in like manner united after the vicissitudes of the pilgrimage in the flesh, and with the good and pure of all ages and climes, in fact of all the worlds of the universe.

When the first joyful greetings and interchange of experiences were fairly over and I could turn my thoughts from the persons among whom I was so gladly received to the conditions of this new life, my curiosity was awakened, and I began to inquire into the nature of the sphere of being upon which I had entered. Evidently we were still in the great universe of nature of which the earth is a part, and of which men in their mortal state have gained some glimpses of knowledge; not in a space set apart beyond the bounds of infinity, and garnished with scenes that were only magnified copies of those familiar on the earth.

As the faculties of the spirit were expanded and untramelled, but not changed in their nature, and as its perceptions were analogous to those which it formerly gained through the senses, so had the surroundings in which it found itself a glorified likeness to those in which it received its first experience and its training for eternal life. And yet, my former conceptions of that life, and of the sphere in which it was destined to pass, now seemed so distorted and inadequate as to be ridiculous. In their aspirations for an immortal state and in their endeavors to picture the glories of the after life, men have of necessity drawn upon their imagination and have used the materials of the existence with which they are familiar. In the various stages of their moral and spiritual development and of their knowledge of the universe, they have painted visions of beauty and delight in accordance with a faith darkened by ignorance and distorted by superstition, regarding as the revelation of supreme wisdom the highest conceptions they could attain. Their heaven was made up of the elements of earth ; their immortal life was a transfiguration of a mortal existence ; and they carried the materials of the dust and the occupations of the flesh into their dreams of a spirit world.

I found that the unlimited expanse of the universe was the home of the disembodied spirit, which could range at will in the wide, free spaces of the heavens. It could indeed visit any of the rolling worlds, which without number peopled the boundless region, but with their actual substance occupied so small a portion of its immensity. By that spiritual power of discernment which corresponds to the vision of the eye, we could take in the grand march of the worlds, as planets circled around their suns, and those suns, with their retinues of shining spheres, moved around greater centres, and those centres again, with their vaster systems, travelled in their appointed circuits. And from these mighty revolutions there came, as it were, a blending of sounds which swept through all the universe in supernal harmony that thrilled the soul with musical delight.

The place which we occupied would appear to human thought to be in the very midst of infinite space—all directions being alike and all distances without limit. While there was no material substance that would be palpable to sense, there were forms and colors perceptible to the spiritual faculties in vivid beauty, constituting scenes of delight and structures of surpassing grandeur, amidst which were the abodes of the blest. While the spirit itself had no substantial embodiment, like that from which it was released by the death of the body, it had a clear individuality, a distinct personality, which was far more fully recognizable by its fellow spirits than it could ever be in the flesh.

There was indeed, a far more vivid perception of personal presence than the embodied soul can know, and a fulness of understanding and a freedom of association impossible in earthly life. If men, imprisoned in the body and dependent upon sense, were to be transported to that celestial scene, the eye would see no form or line of beauty, the ear would hear no sound of joy; and the soul would be shut off from association with the emancipated hosts, seeming to be alone in an infinite void. And yet to the disembodied soul, freed from the trammels of the flesh, the celestial region was filled with glorious brightness and joyous life, and its denizens were occupied with activities to which those of earth were as the torpid movements of the unhatched chrysalis.

Not only did the perceptions far surpass in keenness and clearness those obtained through physical senses, but the sentiments of the soul were exalted and purified, and association was freed from every taint of the passions and selfish instincts derived from an animal state of existence and its necessities. As we reposed amid celestial surroundings we received the effect of grandeur, sublimity, eternal peace, joy-inspiring beauty and melody; or we could move from space to space with the celerity of thought, and join with zest in the manifold activities of the heavenly realm.

The years during which the friend of my earthly days had been separated from me seemed to him like the passage of a night, so absorbed had he been in the delights of the higher state. He told me that he had been gaining in knowledge of the wonders of the universe, and that life was still a continual revelation, and must ever be so. The spirit, new to this state of being, could not grasp its glories all at once, but simply entered upon a new stage of development. As its knowledge grew and its capacities expanded, its power of enjoyment increased, and to the growth of its happiness there was no end.

I could see as we moved about at will

that new marvels everywhere appeared, and that of what there was to learn and to enjoy there could be no possible limit. Not only was the infinite universe open to the exploration of the eager spirit, but its myriads of denizens, gathered from all its parts and brought up from a thousand varied experiences in different spheres and through millions of successive generations, afforded a limitless opportunity for learning by association and communion.

"Tell me," said I, "of this life upon which I have entered, this world so different from what I have been taught to expect. Initiate me into its mysteries."

"Come with me," answered my friend, and no sooner had I given my ready consent than we sped as swift as thought through the infinite realms of space. In a moment's time we seemed to be alone in a part of the heavens far remote from the scene of our meeting. While we reposed in the celestial ether in what seemed a heavenly solitude, though still in the midst of revolving spheres, my friend and teacher began to discourse in answer to my inquiries.

"This is the eternal universe," he began, "the same to which we were introduced at our birth in yonder lowly star, one of the least of these revolving globes; but our comprehension of its nature and wonders while there was almost as imperfect as that of the worm that grovels in its soil. We were then in the midst of this realm of grandeur and of spiritual life, but fastened to one tiny spot with barely vision enough to excite our curiosity and lead us to grope and struggle for more knowledge. All the wisdom that the greatest of men could acquire was but the smallest of beginnings and the faint glimmering of the dawn of truth, whose full day must come in this later life.

"While we were confined to that little planet, though in reality but one among millions and millions of worlds, it seemed to us the central point of all the universe, for which the rest was made to minister, and we were wont to speculate whether that embryonic existence of ours were not all that creation was made for; whether the rest of the universe of which we had a glimpse, was intended for anything but an illumination of our nights; and whether, after we had barely struggled into actual being through that state of spiritual gestation, we did not fall into nothing again,—as if all this grand creation were but the freak of a fantastic Being, without beneficent purpose!

"Even those who had a belief in immortality and fancied that they had attained exalted ideas of the Creator formed from their feeble conjectures and their hopes systems of religious faith which contained only the imperfect germs of the real truth of life and destiny. These, however, were of great value to mankind, putting in form the highest ideals of which they were capable and serving as a nucleus around and upon which they could ever continue to work; and, as they gained in knowledge from the light of reason, they could build more and more beautiful structures of faith, tending toward the symmetry and grandeur of ultimate truth.

"You and I were taught in our childhood to think of a place set apart somewhere in the skies, as the home of departed souls,—a far-off kingdom in the heavens, surrounded perchance with walls like an imperial stronghold, and the abode of winged angels and of the disembodied spirits of the just and good. This celestial realm of which we dreamed was a creation of the imagination of devout poets and ardent mystics wrought from glorified elements of the earthly state. We were told that it contained fields and trees and streams to delight the eye and ear, though the eye and ear were to dissolve and return to dust. We thought of it as having palaces and domes built of the materials with which we were familiar in our mortal state, though these were adapted only to delight through the senses that must depart with the organs of the flesh. It was impossible for us to rise to a conception of an existence above and beyond the need of material forms and objects to minister delight to the soul.

"This earth-like heaven we conceived of as a kingdom in the skies, with orders and regulations modelled after the governments of earth even in its ruder ages; as if the soul were not to attain a state of intelligence and rectitude in which absolute freedom would be its heritage. The notions we were taught to hold of the occupations of the spirit life were like the fancies of childhood, and were the product of the childhood of the race. The noblest conception of the heavenly state was that of white-robed hosts, forever singing praises before the throne of a Sovereign delighting in laudation and glory of himself. Singularly childish was the idea that the Creator of this glorious universe was a being with the personal semblance and attributes of a mighty monarch, seated upon a throne to receive a constant chorus of adulation from a redeemed race, and unending demonstrations of devotion from creatures that he had made.

"Such ideas of the heavenly life grew out of imperfect knowledge and defective reason, but came also from a sincere longing for a state of divine purity and perfection. They were typical of the complete submission and unremitting worship which in human life were felt to be necessary to the attainment of a condition of enduring holiness, and, though wrought from the visions of devout dreamers, became sanctified to the hopes and aspirations of generations of mankind. At the touch of fuller knowledge and sounder reason they fade into a myth, but only to give way to higher conceptions. Now that you have come to the reality you will learn how far it is from the fancies of mankind in their unenlightened days."

IV.

"THE LIFE INDEED."

My friend's discourse was carrying my thoughts back to earth and the errors in which the "little lives of men" are spent, while I wished rather to know of the new life into which I had so suddenly come. He was at once conscious of this feeling on my part; but, in the pause which it had produced, the beloved members of our family, whom we had left in another part of the heavenly space, appeared hovering about us, drawn by the power of sympathy to our presence. My friend needed no questioning from them, but at once explained:

"Our new-comer, like all new-comers, wished to be told, first of all, about the glories of this life by one who has had some experience of them, and as he expressed surprise at finding it so different from the heaven of his earthly dreams, I was beginning to point out the errors into which men have fallen in regard to their destiny. As all this has become familiar to you, we had retired to this solitude for the initiation of his soul into the revelations of the life indeed."

"But why such haste?" responded the sweet voice of my sister. "He will now learn for himself, and as his spiritual experience advances he will only have to turn his thoughts back to understand that life on earth, with all its errors and the problems that seemed so hard to solve. Why interrupt our present joy by going back to it now, even in thought?"

Here our reverend sire interposed. "Aye," he said, "why dwell upon the life you have left behind, and the errors with which men have struggled and are still struggling? The race is hopefully working out its salvation, and as its knowledge widens and deepens, and its reasoning powers attain greater strength through generations of study by the strongest minds, it will more and more come into the light of truth which leads to perfection.

"But now give your thoughts to the life into which you have come, and learn something of your eternal dwelling place. It is all this infinite space, and the disembodied spirit ranges at will among the numberless worlds of the celestial realm. It finds everywhere beauty and joy, in such measure as it is capable of receiving.

"Do not imagine that eternal happiness consists in eternal idleness, or continually singing praises around the throne of an exalted Sovereign; it is found rather in the constant activity of the spirit, in a realm which affords it unlimited scope and inexhaustible fields.

"Death is only a departure from the apparatus of flesh, which was necessary to the embryo state on earth. It is as painless at the last as falling asleep, and the awakening is in a new sphere of life. Of course it works no sudden transformation of character and no instant removal to a place beyond the bounds of the universe. As the soul was before death, so it is after, but freed from the flesh and the feelings and desires engendered by the necessities of the flesh.

"It may be weighed down and overwhelmed almost to numbness and oblivion by the derangement or decay of the mortal vesture before the final dissolution comes, so that it appears to be in darkness and eclipse, but when at last it is loosed from the material bonds, it rises in its full vigor and assumes all the qualities which its origin and earthly experience have given it. As the circumstances of its life, its parentage, early training, education, its own labors and sufferings on earth have made it, so it is well or ill prepared to enjoy the universe of God. But all is before it, infinity of space, eternity of time.

"Upon what is it to exercise its powers, and what is to operate upon its capacities? The infinite state of being! We do not come at once to the knowledge of all things, but must learn. With untrammelled powers, great or small, as the life on earth has left them, with desires lofty or grovelling at the beginning of the spirit life, according as we have acquired or cultivated them, we set forth on the life unlimited. We are in the same school from whose lowest grade we have come, and the subject of study here as there, is the works of God and through them God himself. Our means of learning only are changed.

"We were taught that we should meet God face to face, as mortals on earth may meet a sovereign, in form and lineament like themselves. Nay, God is spirit even as we are spirit; but he is infinite and fills the infinite cosmos with his sole personality, whereas we are finite; and can the finite comprehend the infinite?

"In this life the soul comes into closer communion with the Creator, it learns more and more of his works and thereby gets truer and larger ideas of him; but He is an everlasting mystery, of which we may learn more and more, but which we cannot wholly comprehend till we become infinite in knowledge and capacity, a state toward which we ever advance but unto which we never attain. All the beings in the universe are but a little way advanced from the beginning of this great lesson. The difference between the latest comer and the first man that lived is not great, compared with what lies beyond.

"Here, then, we learn; and behold, how great is the field in which we search for knowledge! All these worlds and systems which man on earth can study slowly and painfully through rude devices of his own contriving, are open to us. We can study them freely, in their motions, in their substance and their contents. We can visit them at will, note their movements, their size, their ingredients, their populations and all that those populations do.

"Think you that the little planet in

yonder small system from which we came, the gem of God's universe, and all the rest a gorgeous setting? Nay, these millions of globes, many of them far greater than the earth, have their inhabitants and their marvels of nature and of art, and as the conditions of each are different from those of the others, the variety has no limit.

"What we have learned of these worlds in the short space since we came to the spirit life is little, but we have visited many, and the more we see, the greater grows the marvel at the variety and extent, beyond all mortal conception a million times multiplied, of the Creator's works and the powers and resources of the infinite Spirit which creates, and which fills and sustains, the mighty cosmos! It is one of the joys of the life eternal to study these works, to know fully things of which we had a glimmering notion on earth, and to find out matters of which we had no conception before.

"Not only have we this universe to explore and study, but here are the millions of disembodied souls with whom we live. Not intellect alone and power of gaining knowledge remain to us, but affections and sentiments, and, above all, that which on earth men call spirituality—which here is, like all else, far more easily active than under the hindrances of the flesh—the native spark of aspiration toward pure, sincere, self-giving growth to noble character. The brotherhood of heaven is vast, the relationship of its members infinitely varied in kind and degree. The communion of spirit with spirit is intimate in proportion as their natures are congenial, and as that communion is intimate, so is the joy that springs from it intense.

"The petty passions and weaknesses that belonged to the flesh are gone, and in every person we can find something to give us new and varied delight, while with some the joy of intercourse is ecstatic. There is here no sham, no deception, no concealment, no misunderstanding. Every spirit is open to the knowledge and the feelings of every other, and all find pleasure in association according to the degree of congeniality. The subjects of discourse, if communion such as you are now experiencing can be called discourse,—this constant interflux of thought and feeling—are infinite and inexhaustible. This is the chief joy of spiritual existence, whether in the body or out of it, this interchange of thought and feeling and the expansion and exaltation that come from it.

"Be sure that here we have our beloved ones; and those who were loved ones on earth hold the first place, though our affections are unconstrained, and fasten upon every object fitted to receive them."

As the paternal spirit paused, again the sister spirit took up her sweet refrain. "And here, too, she said, the ministry of love continues. The occasion has not ceased for helping one another, for sustaining the weak, reclaiming the wayward, and comforting the desolate, but as the passions that pertained to the flesh are gone, and the hard conditions of the earthly life are left behind, the work of love and helpfulness meets quick response and is full of joy."

"But," I exclaimed, "is there no place of punishment for evil-doers, such as we were taught to fear in our childhood?"

"Oh! that terrifying doctrine of a place of torment! I can almost shudder now at the recollection of it!" It was the serene but solemn tone of my mother that uttered this exclamation, and for a moment it continued, like a voice in a revery. "Even the wickednesses of the intelligent and self-indulgent were the stumblings of those afflicted with moral blindness, which a long training in this world of larger light may gradually heal. But the idea that the poor children born in ignorance and sin, growing up amid surroundings in which there was no good influence; or the neglected and untaught, and even the heathen in their mental and moral darkness, were condemned by a righteous God, ever a loving father, to terrible torture! How could a human being with a soul ever believe it!"

"Ah!" replied my friend, "that was one of the many cruel superstitions to which men were subject in time of little knowledge and imperfect reasoning, and which were perpetuated by solemn sanctions for their deterrent effects. The human race, like the human child, has to outgrow its superstitions, and its childhood is long."

V.

THE SECRET OF GROWTH.

Here again the reverend father of our family group of spirits took up the discourse.

"Right and wrong on earth," he said, "are but relative terms. No being ever lived on that sphere who knew all the truth, and it can hardly be said that any ever did, in all respects, exactly the right. The general experience of the race has been made up of gropings toward the true and right, and wanderings from it. Every approach is its own reward, every departure its own punishment. The earthly life of a person is not a thing complete, the account of which is closed up and the compensation weighed out. It is not a whole, but the merest beginning, and the start that some make before death is goodly, while that of others is scarcely a start at all.

"The Almighty saw fit to plant our race there, surrounded by the elements and conditions necessary to growth and development, and then he allowed it to grow and to struggle toward perfection. The elements and conditions were those most likely in the great seasons of eternity to produce the best fruit at last, but in the beginning there must needs be imperfections and partial failures. Some spring forth at once with vigor and beauty, others languish and are stunted; but a soul once struck into separate being from the Infinite, is immortal, and in the eternal years of God shall find the genial warmth that will bring it into bloom.

"Why should God torment the creatures that he has made with greater pains than their own misdoings bring as their natural result? Every misdoing, every departure from the right and true, is followed inevitably by penalty, not measurable by the standards of earthly advantage and disadvantage, but one that has its due effect upon the soul, marring its powers and capacities and sending it to this spirit life by so much unfitted to partake in its joys.

"A soul distorted and deformed by the experiences of earth, is an object of pity, not of wrath, and here it is taken tenderly in charge by happier spirits, and everything is done to make up for the disadvantages and misfortunes of the life below. Such souls find their punishment, if punishment it may be called, in their power to see what they have lost, and to comprehend what they might enjoy but do not; but before them lies the eternal life with its wider opportunities and its greater helps. The loss may be made up and some spirits that came here from utter wretchedness and degradation are now among the most resplendent and joyous, the more so for the sufferings they have passed through.

"If the great scheme of that embryo

life is such that a soul may come into it impressed through the medium of its birth with bad tendencies, which are confirmed and strengthened by surroundings and experience, with no good influences brought to bear to overcome them, and that soul becomes what it inevitably must become under those circumstances, does it not thereby suffer a terrible penalty for holding its place in the world and serving, even in that hapless position, to help carry out the general plan of development; and is the God that made him and put him there to be offended and subject him to further torture to satisfy a " divine anger"? Is anger ever divine?

"Nay, rather, will not the poor being that comes halting hither from hard places in the human life be tenderly cherished, taught what he never before had a chance to learn, made to see what never before came to his blinded vision, helped to gain what he has missed, and gradually brought to enjoy the bliss intended for all? His was a hard lot and here he finds compensation; for his bliss, when gained, seems the sweeter, inasmuch as it was gained so late and after so much bitterness.

"That notion of a 'systematic' and eternal punishment of those so unfortunate as to wander far from the right, is a relic of the horrible idea of God, which was the conception of an early generation, as an all-powerful Being that becomes enraged at disobedience to his commands, and will subject to the torment those that dare disregard his law.

"The figures of Oriental speech, the stern doctrine uttered by the warning prophets of Ancient Israel, and scraps of the mythology of Babylon and Persia, are the materials from which apocalyptic writers of early days and ardent preachers of later time wrought the horrible hell in which souls were doomed to suffer endless pains in eternal fires. The material hell of fire and torment was one of the hideous myths of the superstitious ages, sanctified by earnest but misguided teachers of later times. It had deterrent horrors only for the ignorant and superstitious, since the disembodied spirit could not suffer from darkness and fire, from heat or cold, which operate only upon the senses of the flesh.

"The worst of this hideous myth was the effect it had upon the conception of God, making him a monster of cruelty. Could a spirit, infinite in goodness as in power, devise such a horrid pit for such a fiendish purpose? And where in this goodly universe should it be placed? The superstitious idea of heaven and hell would put them both outside the universe, beyond the bounds of infinity, and leave all that is or can be in existence of no use or value through eternity.

"And then there was that horrid phantasm, the Devil, which the mind of man conjured up to divide the empire of creation with its Maker! Rude and ignorant people were always disposed to account for wrongs and misfortunes, real or seeming, by attributing them to the workings of evil spirits. The old Hebrew race on earth was more free than most primitive people from this form of superstition, and it was from the exile in Assyrian and Babylonian lands that the Israelites brought back the notion of an adversary of Jehovah. It was derived from the Persian mythology of Ormuzd and Ahriman, the conflict of light and darkness, of good and evil, for the possession of the world and of man. Out of this borrowed notion of Satan and the dreams of apocalyptic seers grew the fantastic devil-lore with which Christianity became disfigured.

"A place of everlasting torment, tenanted by evil spirits who go abroad in the world tempting and enticing men to destruction, was a product of superstition which knowledge and reason alone could dispel. Even in recent times, when large numbers of Christian believers have thrown away the self-convicting absurdity of a physical hell for spiritual beings, the terrors of a place or state of everlasting spiritual torment has replaced the cruder creed. But this, too, is as foolishly inconsistent with all the 'fatherly' conceptions of the Deity which they accept from the teachings of Jesus, as was the paradox of bodily burning for a disembodied spirit.

"On the earth which we have left, the time comes on apace when mankind shall see with fuller knowledge and clearer reason, and the myths of the later theologies shall be cast out like the outgrown superstitions of the earlier ages. They have been cherished long because of the sanctions of ancient faith and the tendency of generation after generation to accept the beliefs transmitted from the past and sanctified by the wise and good in their time. The imaginations of men have been wont to regard the ancients and the fathers as if their wisdom accumulated with time, whereas the present is always the maturest age. The ancient world was young. The modern world is older. The latest result of man's knowledge and thought is ever nearest to the eternal truth."

"Doubtless," I said, "men are still far from the truth in matters of physical science and philosophy as well as in matters that pertain to their spiritual relations?"

"They are far from the ultimate truth," was the reply, "and they can never reach it under the limitations of the earthly life. Even after they have escaped from those limitations, they can only advance toward it with ever-increasing enlightenment. But the human intellect from its first awakening began to grope toward the light, and the spiritual instinct has constantly struggled toward the truth."

VI.

DISCOURSE OF A HEAVENLY SAGE.

Just at this point in the discourse of my beloved father, we became keenly conscious of the presence with us of another spirit of most benign and venerable aspect. He was indeed a seer among the spirits in the part of the universe to which I had been drawn by the presence of my loved ones. He had been a dweller upon the earth in a far distant time and was wise above his fellows, but more than 2000 years ago he had left his mortal state and had been a denizen of the world of spirits, as I presently learned. Diffusing by his mere presence the influence of benignant wisdom, and begetting in others a profound sentiment of respect and a desire to learn of him, this sage of the heavens spoke to us; and what can only be characterized to earthly understanding as the tones of his voice thrilled our being with the charm of immortal music.

"My children," he began, "ye are plainly just from Earth and that dim life in which the soul begins. Learn from one who was deemed a philosopher there many centuries before you saw the light, and in the interval here—so long in the computations of men, so brief in the reckoning of God—has still explored the mysteries of life with unceasing zest.

"Think not that ye can search at once the Infinite Soul of the universe and understand His working from the beginning. The soul that was first rounded into a separate being in the chrysalis of flesh, and first let loose as an ever-living spirit in this realm of endless progress, is far from comprehending all the ways of God. In Him we live and in Him we grow to larger knowledge, to higher wisdom, to stronger love; but to infinite capacity the finite being can never reach.

"The Infinite Soul made not the universe. He is the universe. It is wrought out of His being. Forth from his creative power came the substance of all the material worlds, and in that substance wrought the power that gave it forth. According to the laws of wisdom and of love it wrought, whirling into form the essence of the worlds to be, and setting at work the forces that should impart to them the all-pervading life. To this creative energy and its laws of action, what was duration—as conceived by the finite mind? Through the silent epochs it lived in the substance which had been evolved from itself, bringing it into form and order. From the all-pervading ether the substance was brought into nebulous masses, the subtile material of the celestial systems that were to come.

"In these nebulous masses wrought with force of heat and motion the untiring life, and they took form and grew to plastic substance. Along the lines of plan and purpose still wrought the soul of all, making of plastic substance suns and solid worlds, cast by force of heat and motion into form and order. The informing life on lines of law immutable set spheres and systems on their way, and hung the universe with stars. Not all at once, as with touch of magic wand or by theatric fiat, but in due process of evolution,—the creative Spirit working along the laws of its infinite being in the substance it had made,—the cosmic universe came into orderly being and activity.

"From plastic form to solid grew the spheres, with wild combustion of their elements but with the eternal purpose working through all their ferment, till the conditions of the coming life were wrought upon them. Life was in them moving ever towards its aim. With all-persistent energy, not blind and headlong Force from naught evolved, but the Soul Divine, in might and wisdom working, brought the roaring elements, subject to its will and purpose, into harmonious interaction. On new-formed worlds the creative spirit wrought by thrilling heat in proto-plasmic slime, and infused vitality to bring forth living things, monstrous plants and animals, to be each other's sustenance and prepare the way for higher forms as new conditions served.

"The life in these was life of God, the only life, by methods of the divine will working toward its mighty end, to people the universe with spirits, offspring of itself. Through ages, epochs, æons,—the seasons of the universe's one great harvest,—the process moved. From lower forms the divine gestation wrought to higher, till worlds were clothed with beauty and filled with life. From out each other generations grew, evermore tending to perfection, each becoming material for the next, in one creative process. The all-informing Spirit from species wrought to species, combining forms and forms dividing, evolving qualities and itself infusing more and more.

"At last upon the earth, whence we have come, and upon other spheres in his vast universe, the all-pervading God brought forth, from generation after generation of lower forms, the upright shape of man. Towards this had tended all the work of creative energy. The Infinite Soul had wrought to embody finite souls and impart the ever-living spirit to separate beings that should dwell at last and dwell forever in this wide realm of space, the objects of eternal and unbounded love and with capacities for love unlimited.

"Nor was the race of God's children created in perfection, or the soul at once imbued with the Divine Father's attributes. The creative spirit that from formless substance evolved the worlds, and on the worlds the forms of beauty and the abodes of life, and into varied forms its own life infused, still wrought in men to evolve the being that should be capable of the destiny that was from the beginning creation's purpose. Through all progressive purpose ran. The instincts of life, to light and heat responsive, that first appeared in plants, rose in animals into sense, with gleams of intelligence and of sentiment, to serve the ends of their being; and still these instincts wrought from lower on to higher forms, till the spirit was lighted at the flame of growing mind and stronger feeling. Generation out of generation came, with many a lapse of living unto dead and extinction of the taper-lights of starting souls, until the flame grew self-sustaining.

"Here and there creative power set alight a torch that drew souls upward and inspired the race of men to mighty strides of progress, far above its brutish origin. Thought began its work within the brain, language was devised to carry it on from brain to brain, and recorded history set up its monuments that time to come might derive aid from time gone by, and man could make his way toward his destiny. Did God recede from out His work and leave the children he had made to stumble onward to their fate? Nay, as his all-pervading spirit had been in the void heavens, in the whirling mass of formless substance, in the evolving worlds, and in the clothing life thereon, so was it working still in the race of man to bring it to perfection.

"Upon our little earth, what has history been, and what experience, but the growth of men through processes of evolution, wherein the revelation of God is to be read with ever-growing clearness? As in the process of evolving man from beast, the incipient soul, the flickering spirit, in the mere flame of vital force involved, lapsed into extinction with the body's death, serving but to kindle the generations to a higher glow until the soul could live apart from physical life, so hath God still wrought within the race of man to bring forth perfect souls, offspring of himself and fit to abide with him,—objects of infinite love, which wrought through all to this sole end. Immortal spirits by process of selection and survival from this human race have sprung, and ever it tends to rise to where all its souls shall that degree attain of freedom from the brute and from the long inheritance of death, by which they can live apart from flesh and sense,—that family of the Eternal God, for which creative power hath been exerted through all the ages.

"This orderly evolution, which is the Divine method, the progressive effect of the Infinite Mind seeking its constant aim, producing creative results through laws that finite minds can grasp and rise upon, is not yet complete on that small planet, where we erstwhile dwelt, nor in the universe at large. Behold the little way that man has crept from his ancestral brute, save the few high souls that have received God's light to diffuse among their kind!

"See how, at the dawn of recorded history, the brutish instincts still prevailed, and passions derived from the animal life and meant to spur it on to higher development, overcame the qualities of the struggling soul. Man saw in wind and storm, in light and dark, and in the process of earth's elements his God, and in terror made Him one or many, in imagination compassed round with invisible powers benign or malignant; but the serene Soul that wrought in love and wisdom was to him unknown. Man cast into forms visible or fanciful the gods he feared, and worshipped them in dread, not love, to turn away their wrath or gain their favor. From his own dim soul he made a soul to him divine, gave it the passions of his body and called it God. Hence gross or fierce, man's earliest deity.

"Then how raged the passions of the incipient soul, tumultuous qualities of ancestral brutes, mingling in overwhelming force with the Spirit Divine now making way in man! From this creative ferment, —the process still from which the perfect race should spring,—came bloody wars, the rise and fall of states, destruction of races, and new races rising forth to greater heights, and all the while men made their gods in image of themselves, and in them worshipped themselves to godly stature magnified.

"Yet in the growing race 'twas God that wrought, his spirit more and more infusing into the souls of men, and bringing more and more the heart into subjection. It was evolution still, the eternal Spirit working in material substance toward its destined end, to bring immortal souls into separate being, and establish mutual love between the infinite Soul and its myriad offspring. 'Twas more of God within man's soul that raised one or another o'er his fellows and made him leader, teacher, prophet, to bring his people up to higher, grander and purer light.

"One while and in one region of the earth arose in man the spirit of conquest and of power, developing the force to overcome and bring into subjection to the will. Another while and otherwhere pervailed the spirit of law to bring into order and safe system the body politic and social; from this came ever-growing germs of just and stable government. Again, arose the intellect to lofty flights in thought and reason, reaching after wider, deeper knowledge and higher truth; and love of beauty and of symmetry sought expression in works of art and skill, emulating the great Creator's handiwork. Again, the Divine spirit that wrought upon the earth inspired a people, for that end chosen, with sentiments of pure love for parent and child, for kin and race, for the Power above but dimly known and felt, and instilled the sense of reverence and obedience. From this sprang family love, the patriot's ardor, and purified affection, with sense of right o'ermastering the tendency to wrong. Still wrought the striving soul to overcome the brute in man, the inheritance of the primal stage.

"As elements of the growing race developed thus in varied time and place, the period of their commingling came, and ere the contact of ingredients, attractive and repellent, was brought about for the fierce ferment, within the bosom of the mass arose the sweet leaven of self-denying love and of the devotion of one to other's good, which through long turmoil of conflict should ever spread with regenerating force, to bring at last the good and pure to mastery of the powers of ill,—not ill in God's great plan but incidental ill to man in process of his growth.

"Lo! through generations still the ferment goes. From its commotion have nations sprung to greater height from other nations' ruin, and institutions grown, sloughing off the old, outworn devices of a weaker time, and with vital energies of the rising race adapting all to newer needs. The intellect of man, inventive and contriving, or in reflection calmly reasoning, with ever growing zeal seeks for knowledge and for power to serve his race and make all forces minister to its wants. But also grows the sense of right, the love of beauty and of truth, the aspiration for the higher state to which the soul hath felt itself the destined heir since first divinity became a conscious element within its depths.

"On many spheres the contest still goes on, with varied strides of progress, the contest through which the embodied spirit surmounts the impulses of the flesh, derived from that long ancestry of the brute through which the soul has climbed and grown in power till fit to be let loose for life without the flesh. A contest, viewed by the finite mind, but in truth no contest, for in all is but the steady working of the one great Soul, to the end of peopling heaven with its offspring. Nor deem that perfection yet is reached when souls are born to heavenly life through throes of death from forth the dark gestation of the earth. 'Tis life begun, not finished."

VII.

LIFE ON A DISTANT SPHERE.

The thrilling influence of the benign spirit ceased and the glow of his presence was withdrawn. From one to another among our congenial group the vibrations of his wisdom passed, begetting reflections that were as fully reciprocal as if we had made them subject of discussion. In this soothing contemplation of the meaning of the message and this silent communion of sympathetic souls, we reposed as it were upon beds of invisible and impalpable down, until at length my thoughts were diverted to the vast array of worlds and systems that make up the material universe, discernible to the spiritual vision in all its limitless extent. Half musing I inquired: "And all these rolling spheres that circle around their many suns, are they peopled with beings like the inhabitants of the earth?"

It was not so much an inquiry demanding answer as an expression of wonder, but my beloved friend promptly replied: "Those myriad spheres are at various stages of development and decay, from the nebulæ seething with the germs of life, to the worn out planet lapsing into its original elements through the exhaustion of the forces of light and heat. Upon many of them are races of people like the inhabitants of earth in being the creatures of the same God, owing the same duties to themselves and to Him, but in each world they differ in their surroundings, in the conditions of life and the degrees of progress which they have made in working out their own perfection.

"There is one world, remote from that part of the heavens in which our mortal existence was passed, which I chiefly love to visit. I came upon it in one of the explorations which I am fond of making among the distant spheres, and was attracted by its likeness to a larger and more perfect earth. It seemed to me that *there* was what philosophers had so long dreamed that human life might be, after ages more of experiment with diminishing failure and growing success,—a sort of ideal state in which man's mastery over nature and over himself had become well-nigh complete. I will not attempt to tell you of this world and the state of its people, but you shall see for yourself."

Then with no other effort than the exercise of volition, our whole group, almost wrapped in each other's being, like a single soul, removed from where we had been reposing in the ethereal solitude, and glided through the heavens, swift or slow as the spirit willed. We were conscious of the passage of other spirits on various journeys and of groups reposing in bowers that would be invisible to eyes of flesh, but to the spiritual vision were resplendent with beauty.

We passed worlds and systems of worlds until at last we drew near a planet that revolved with others around one of the brightest suns of the firmament, but one which no optical instrument had ever brought within the ken of mortals on the earth. When we reached the soft atmosphere that wrapped this world about, we paused and glided slowly over it as it floated calmly on its way.

It was a globe of about twice the diameter of the earth, similarly situated with reference to its sun and having similar motions, but with longer days and seasons. About it hung twelve moons of different sizes and at different distances. From the surface of the planet these seemed to occupy different parts of the sky, and as they reflected the light of the sun in their various positions were in different stages of change and therefore diverse in apparent shape. The heavens, seen through the soft and lucid atmosphere, were wonderfully rich in brightness and glory, and must have exerted a peculiarly exalting influence on the people of that happy sphere.

As we came nearer, I observed that the surface of the planet was made up of land and water in varied forms. There were mountains and valleys and plains, oceans in which the land seemed to be floating, lakes and streams like glittering gems and shining bands. Hence there were clouds and rain and storm.

Then I thought of the words of the heavenly seer and clearly saw that all the worlds were of one substance, similar combinations of the same elements, on which, under the effect of heat and motion in their multitudinous forms, similar varieties of life had been engendered. I understood how in the far-off beginning they had been one mass in which the creative Spirit began its work, that work going on through æons, which to God are as nothing and to man as an eternity; the substance was thrown asunder by centrifugal force and distributed in separate masses through infinite space, and these in due time subdivided into worlds and systems.

I seemed to follow the great process, as in the silent ages through the lonely heavens the creative Spirit wrought, as these worlds were fitted for organic life, and as organic life began upon them. I saw the conditions of the worlds change under the operation of this mighty power at work through them all, new and higher forms of life appearing until the sentient, thinking being sprang forth—a newborn intelligence, an individual soul emanating from the great pervading Soul of all, and immortal as Itself.

My companions were aware of these thoughts, and my friend recalled me from my speculations to the object of our visit.

"The beings that inhabit this world," he said, "seem to have had more favorable conditions and a longer experience than the race to which we belonged. At all events they are much farther advanced toward a perfect state.

"Their early history is involved in obscurity like all other early history, and what they have of it themselves is mixed with vague traditions and conjectures. To the Divine Mind it is all clear, but we finite spirits can only study what is, and reason back to what was and forward to what will be."

We glided about this globe with the quickness of thought but with a celerity and accuracy of perception which enabled us closely to note its appearance and peculiarities. I saw that the people had completely overcome the obstacles of nature and established means of communication over its entire surface. The contour of land and water was such that at some point or other the continents approached each other within a few miles. Near these narrow straits the climate might have been forbidding and the nature of the country originally inhospitable, but the appliances which the people had brought to bear in the course of long generations had overcome these disadvantages.

No parts of the planet were given up to wilderness or desert, but labor had brought the wilderness into subjection and made the desert like a garden, to minister to the wants of the people. Art had also been used to moderate the extremes of climate and to protect the person from their effects, so that every portion of that globe was accessible and serviceable to its inhabitants. Every part was made to minister to every other part by means of rapid and constant intercommunication.

The people had by long study acquired a complete knowledge of the outlines and the heights and depressions of the land, whether above the water or in the depths of the sea, and along all convenient lines were roads, on the surface, through mountain ranges, over rivers, straits and lakes, or under the ground or water, according to requirement. Roads for travel and for freight transportation were separate, and on each were cars or carriages exactly fitted for every purpose and every convenience, and propelled with such velocity that the circuit of the planet could be compassed in a single day.

On these lines of communication the people and their merchandise passed to and fro constantly. Oceans caused no delay, for these roads ran to the narrow passages and crossed them by bridge or tunnel without interruption. The bottom of the ocean, too, in its widest part, was traversed by the travelling devices of these people, their ingenuity having contrived such swift means of locomotion and such effectual methods of supporting life beneath the water, that even this great obstacle had been overcome.

I learned from my friend, who had often visited this world, that all the forces of nature had been pressed into service to supply the most effective motive power. Not only electricity, but also the expansive force of many solid, liquid and gaseous substances, the force of gravitation, power of their solar light, the motion of the planet itself, and all the active powers of the elements had been harnessed to the engines of this wonderful people.

But their travel was not confined to the solid ground. The surface of the water was traversed for purposes of pleasure and of traffic in vessels fitted with every convenience for comfortable living and such perfect apparatus and safeguards that danger was never thought of. These vessels moved swiftly or slowly like living things controlled by the will of the navigator.

Not only the land and the sea bore the people hither and thither with wonderful speed, perfect safety and exact precision, but the air, too, was filled with vessels that seemed to fly like animated creatures. Single persons were borne about, hundreds of feet above the ground in all directions by a simple contrivance that sped like a bird whithersoever the occupant directed it, and large companies sailed in gay aerial ships that obeyed their pilot's wish as to speed and direction, and went over mountain-tops and seas.

Not only in temperate and tropic climes did these vessels ply, but they passed over frozen seas and lands, disembarking their passengers, if they so willed, among the icebergs at the very poles. Everywhere they carried devices adapted to the place, heating or cooling the atmosphere, keeping off moisture or relieving dryness, according to the requirements of the case.

My friend told me, moreover, that they had burrowed beneath the surface of the ground, travelling to and fro in its depths and sending merchandise long distances through subterranean tubes with marvellous speed.

Besides all these methods of swift travel they had a complete system for the communication of speech over all the surface of the planet, so that messages could be sent in an instant from one point to another, however far apart. All lines for the transmission of messages were beneath the surface or within the buildings, so that the apparatus did not attract the eye or stand in the way, and instruments connecting with them were in every house. The ingenuity of the people had overcome every obstacle to freedom of movement and communication, and they had become one great brotherhood, constantly mingling together and in close association to the very limits of their world. They understood how completely their interests were one, and every clime and land ministered freely to every other, exchanging products and advantages of every kind.

There was but one language spoken, and that was formed and perfected in the process of ages from the choicest elements of all the tongues that had originally come into use in various regions, and therefore was the most consummate medium for expressing thought that thought itself could devise.

Observing still more closely, we could see that the same ingenuity which had devised such perfect means of travel and transportation had been able to utilize all the resources and forces of nature in supplying the wants of the people. Every clime and every land was devoted to the labor and the production for which it was best adapted, and means were used to extract from each the richest results, without wasting its strength. The soil was made to yield up its best treasures freely. Where there was too much moisture means were found to remove it; where there was not enough, it was supplied. The temperature was regulated according to the wants of the farmer or gardener, and he was the master and not the slave of the elements. All his work for which force was necessary was performed by the forces of nature. He only planned and directed, furnishing the intelligence needed to secure the best results. Each locality being devoted to the production of those things for the growth of which it was best fitted, and every appliance being used to obtain its treasures in the fullest abundance, there was no waste of effort, and these riches were constantly distributed and interchanged so as to keep every want of all the people supplied.

In the cultivation of the soil attention was not given solely to fruits and grains to satisfy the animal wants, but every variety of trees and shrubs and flowers that could delight the eye and give beauty to the landscape, was planted and fostered with judgment and artistic taste. Neither did industry busy itself exclusively on the surface, but the riches of the rocks and of the seas were made accessible. They were not sought with the feverish eagerness which prevailed when they were found with difficulty and in meagre quantities ages before, for now the storehouses were opened and what was wanted could be had at any time.

Beneath the mountains and hills were mines and shafts cutting through the vaults in which their riches were hid, and in these were all appliances for obtaining the stores of gems and metals. Those that were useful in the manifold arts of life were in constant demand, and men were at work getting them out, but nobody cared to accumulate them for their own sake.

The wealth that was scattered in the caves and valleys of the sea had also been brought within reach. The depths, once given up to solitude and the grisly monsters of the under-world, were explored by the active beings who had asserted their mastery over the planet and its possessions. They had appliances which enabled them to live long at the bottom of the oceans and to travel their depths at will; and whatever was hidden there that could serve them for ornament or use they sought out and brought to the light.

So perfect were the appliances for travel and transportation that the people were distributed over the face of the planet exactly in accordance with their tastes and wishes, for whatever any one wanted he could easily obtain, no matter how far from the source of supply. While concentration and co-operation in the various interests and enterprises of life created centres of business and of population, there were no densely crowded cities.

Wherever the convenience of commerce or any other consideration placed these centres of life and activity, there the markets and warehouses were clustered together in proximity to wharves and depots, which were furnished with all manner of mechanical contrivances for loading and unloading merchandise and transporting it from point to point. Very little muscular force of man or animal was used about the docks and storehouses, so manifold were the appliances of mechanism. Every building was exactly suited to its purpose in location and character, and there was no interference or clogging in the broad avenues.

There was no occasion to economize space, since in moving back and forth time is the important consideration, and they had means of passing long distances in short periods. Hence there were broad spaces about all the buildings and the thoroughfares were ample, giving perfect freedom of movement. Near the depots and stores in concentric circles were all manner of factories and shops in which every article that the people might want could be found, but no dwellings were placed in proximity to these establishments of traffic. Spread for miles around along diverging avenues were the habitations of the people, each occupying ample space, with fruitful gardens and shaded walks and a profusion of rich herbage and trees and flowers. Each home was filled with comfort, and surrounded by the influences that refine and elevate, but there was no outward sign of luxury or extravagance.

These people had learned generations before that there was no true happiness in luxury, no enjoyment in parade; and after fierce struggles and perverse opposition, had accepted the great lesson that the results of the united labors of the community belonged of right to that community for the satisfaction of the rational wants of every member. No man was regarded as having any right to a superfluity while another was in need. That great lesson once learned, poverty, ignorance and crime soon departed from the world, for enough is easily obtained from nature's bounty to minister to every reasonable need of body and mind. And, poverty and ignorance once banished, crime and vice speedily disappeared.

Another beneficent result of the wisdom attained by this people was that there was no longer any waste of labor. Every individual did his share of work, so that there were no consumers who did not help gather in the supplies, no drones supported by others' work: neither was there any throwing away of the products of nature and of labor after they had been obtained.

In their old barbaric ages, as in the

present of worlds still in their infancy, the recklessness and wantonness of the people were constantly destroying their possessions. Fire was allowed to burn them up, disasters on land and sea swept them to fragments and to nothingness, waves devoured them, and ignorance was continually throwing precious things into heaps of rubbish.

Now there was no rubbish. Everything was utilized from the moment it came from the bosom of nature till it returned thither to nourish new growths, and nowhere in the cycle of transformation was it permitted to become noxious or useless. Wholesomeness, cleanliness and beauty accompanied all the operations of nature under the wise direction of man.

Another great lesson which this people had learned in their ages of experience was that it was folly, absolute and without mitigation, to spend all one's days and wear out life in accumulating what can at best be but partially used, and that only as a means of promoting the real objects of existence.

Those things which in the rude old times were treasured as wealth and held as precious for their own sake—what were they but the means of securing the conditions of comfortable life, and how small a share could one man profitably use! Yet thousands were wont to toil throughout their lives in heaping together, what they with unconscious irony of truth called "means," while those real ends, for which the means ought to have been used, were overlooked and forgotten. Not only did those who made themselves rich, by grasping such a large share of the gifts of nature, multiply their own labor and trouble without benefit to themselves, but they were engaged in a cruel struggle to keep those gifts from the possession of others, thereby causing misery to their fellow-beings. Now they had learned that this selfish spirit destroyed their own happiness.

No one cared longer for great accumulations. Every one had all he needed or desired, and used it to secure the means of real happiness by promoting the development of his own character and gratifying his noblest tastes, while finding it essential to his happiness also to see that others had an opportunity of doing the same thing. The real purpose of life was now understood, and that blindness was no longer known which had mistaken the means of living for its object. To supply all the actual wants of the people required but a small share of the time and effort of each individual, devoted to that special end.

I found that not over one-sixth of everybody's time was spent in productive labor. In the system of industry which brought the treasures of nature from her stores to the places and the persons that needed them, and in the form and condition which made them most useful, every person took his part, but the whole work was easily and fully accomplished by the devotion of one-sixth of each person's time to the work. Every one did a certain part according to his aptitude and capacity or the circumstances of his life, and every one received, with all the precision that comes from obeying the laws of nature and of justice, his due share of the results.

VIII.

PROGRESS OF A PERFECT RACE.

Of my friend,—who had learned much of the history of this people, not only by circulating unseen among them and making those rapid observations and ready inferences which only the disembodied spirit is capable of, but by communion with those who had passed their mortal state upon that sphere,—I asked by what process the present industrial condition had been attained; whether through what we had known as communism or socialism, or any other device of public regulation.

"Nay," he replied, "this state of comparative perfection has been attained by growth and development in individual character, and by getting into practice, after generations of experience and increasing wisdom, the principles of justice and beneficence through the voluntary co-operation of the people. Where every one is willing to do his share of work and capable of understanding what his share is; where each one is content with his share of the result, and where all are ready, even anxious, to give others an equal chance with themselves and accord to each that to which he is entitled, there is no longer any ground for troubles and difficulties. Where intelligence and an absolute sense of right prevail, and where personal selfishness is displaced by a devotion to the general good, co-operation becomes easy and effective in every branch of activity and between different branches over the widest domain. The methods and agencies of such a co-operation are readily found and applied, and they work with the harmony that necessarily comes from obedience to moral laws."

"But," I said, "capacities being different and employments varying, how are the results fairly apportioned? Surely each one does not receive the same share of the products of the common labor."

"Surely not," was the reply. "You must remember that the state of things we see here is the result of generations of development and growth, of long ages of experience and discipline in the virtues, but through it all has wrought the spirit of emulation and the spur of a stimulus to effort. It has not produced a flat level of uniformity in these beings or the inanition of a life devoid of motives to exertion. But great is the power of justice directed by intelligence, and mighty is the sway of the principle of unselfishness, once accepted and all-prevailing. The men who form the vast community peopling this beautiful planet vary in their qualities and capacities, but they have learned to recognize the responsibilities and obligations of their varying talents.

"Through their voluntary system of coöperation each one receives a share in the product of the common effort exactly proportioned to his part in the work of production, including all the processes of distribution. This has become very simple and easy from the fact that every one in his relation with others fully understands what he is entitled to and what others are entitled to, and every one is perfectly satisfied with his own and willing to accord to others that which is fairly theirs. The ancient contentions and tribulations were due to selfishness and ignorance, and the thousand wrongs that flowed from them."

"Then," I said, "there must be the rich and the comparatively poor among these people, the wise and the comparatively simple, with differences of station and conditions of life."

"Well," said the spirit, with serene gravity, "if there were not, what would be the use of continuing this mortal existence upon a material globe? The race might as well be disembodied at once, for it would have no further use for this material field of effort and of training. But, long ago, those of superior capacity learned that they exercised a stewardship for the benefit of others. The community did not claim or seize the products of labor, skill and prudence to hold them in common and distribute them equally, thus destroying the springs of benevolence and the motives of mutual helpfulness, and drawing the very life-blood of progress. But those to whom much was given gave much. What came to them as the result of superior wisdom and capacity, they turned back in rich measure upon the community. Not only did they see justice done in all matters with which they were concerned, but, where need was, they contributed generously to mitigate the evils that came from imperfect conditions, and thereby to remedy those conditions. They wrought wisely with their means and their ability, to dispel poverty and crime and suffering, to suppress the evils that afflicted their race and to remove the causes of evil, to educate, to enlighten and to elevate.

"It is largely by this process—of devoting wealth obtained by individual effort to promoting the common well-being—that the present comparatively perfected state of things was reached. Fresh from earthly experience, you can well imagine that the process was long, but that, once begun, it grew constantly easier and more rapid, as the ratio of light to darkness increased. So long as there were wrongs to be corrected, evils to be remedied and needs to be supplied, the capable gave of their efforts and the rich of their substance in a beneficent co-operation for the amelioration of the race.

"For a long time now this plan of beneficence has been working until ignorance, poverty, wickedness and suffering have been exterminated, by no system of laws and regulations, but by an all-pervading spirit of mutual helpfulness and generous co-operation, which enforces its own decrees. Like every great result, it has come through *growth*. All are maintained in comfort and ease by systems of industry and interchange, gradually devised and voluntarily carried on, and regulated by the natural principles of justice and right-doing. All *opportunities* are made equal, and those who by superior capacity attain a large share of wealth make it part of their business to provide for the general needs and for the embellishments of life, not for themselves alone but for the community at large, seeking to diffuse with wisely directed beneficence the advantages which they enjoy. The difference between public and private interests and methods is well-nigh obliterated by the constant and universal application of the principles of unselfishness, and all see how much better off and how much happier they are for it."

As our family party of celestial visitants continued to explore this scene of mortal life in its wonderfully developed phases, from observation and the comments of our guide I learned more and more how the time was passed by these fortunate beings. As I have said, not more than one-sixth of the hours of each day were devoted by any person to his share of regular labor. The rest of the time was spent in living. It was divided by old and young in due proportions—not by regulation but by natural aptitude and good sense—between repose and activity; including study and the acquisition of knowledge, observation, and the interchange of thought and ideas, rational sports, and pure enjoyments. It was plainly a life of comfort and happiness from which the taint of suffering and sorrow had been eliminated.

For purposes of education there were schools, museums containing specimens of all products of nature and of human skill, art-galleries, collections of all things useful or beautiful. During the hours of each day devoted to education these objects were studied and made familiar in all their characteristics. Libraries, which were the daily resort of the people, were filled with the thoughts and the wisdom of the great, whether living or dead, but nothing worthless, nothing which was not calculated to contribute to the growth and perfection of the soul was admitted to them. In fact, long ago the minds of these people had ceased to be employed in creating worthless literature, and what had been created of that kind had fallen into oblivion and gone to dust. There was no longer any demand for such productions. All means of culture were provided by the people, and ever open for the free use of all.

Every appliance that could be devised for the promotion of the health and happiness of the people—great parks, with their walks and drives, their lakes and fountains, their fields, groves and bowers for the diversion and enjoyment of old and young—had been provided out of the wealth of the community, not by any public levy but by voluntary contributions from those whose incomes were largest. In the same way indoor establishments for diversion and healthful sports and exercises, and for all manner of amusements were maintained, and still are maintained, by co-operation of private means and efforts. The care and management of all such appliances for the general benefit are in the hands of competent persons employed by the associations that support them. There is no need of the intervention of public authority, which indeed hardly exists as authority.

"But can it be," I asked of my guide and friend, "that here is a mortal race which has outgrown the vices, wrongs and sufferings still so familiar to human beings on the earth?"

"Almost," was the reply. "Here is a people in which all the primal differences of race and blood have become blended into a common brotherhood, and a common sympathy and sound fellow-feeling have taken the place of old antipathies. Through the discipline of past experience and the growth of wisdom they have learned that to work together for the general good is the best means of promoting the individual well-being. They have learned to conform their lives to the laws of nature and the principles of right, and thereby they avoid the ills that spring from disease and misfortune.

"The greatest progress toward this state of immunity from what used to be called the 'ills of life' was made when first the people came fully to appreciate the importance of birth. They learned that the struggle to correct inherited tendencies and innate impulses was well-nigh futile, and saw the wisdom of a sound start in life. Hence they began to give attention to pre-natal influences and conditions, and to avoid the propagation of physical, mental and moral defects. A few generations of that kind of prudence wrought wonderful results upon the race, and what used to be regarded as natural depravity, —qualities transmitted from a far-off brute origin,—rapidly disappeared.

"As offspring became the result of rational purpose instead of blind impulse, it was easier to train it to a wholesome development, but in that process wisdom was still applied at every step. As the intellect and moral sense opened to surrounding influences they were wisely and gently directed, and children almost unconsciously formed right habits of conduct and sound views of their relations in life. The animal instincts, once so strong and so prone to vice, were overcome by the careful development of higher qualities, and evil tendencies were neutralized and progressively excluded by the occupation of the mind with noble thoughts and pure sentiments. Under the process of wise and tender parental training the old anxieties of families were displaced with unalloyed domestic felicity.

"As the result of health in body and mind, produced by sound birth and wholesome influences, these men and women are exquisite in beauty of form and feature, and buoyant with unvarying cheerfulness. They are clad, as you will observe, in simple garments, calculated to promote their comfort, and to set off rather than to conceal the grace and symmetry of the body. They long ago lost the taste for artificial adornments, for when physical defects had been overcome they found that natural beauty was far more attractive without these."

Here I suggested that with us on earth unwise or imprudent marriages had been the cause of many evils difficult to deal with.

"Yes," my friend replied, "and this race went through a like experience in ages past. Before ignorance and folly in regard to such all-important relations had been overcome by enlightenment, men and women were incited by impulses arising from their physical nature to unions in which wisdom had no part. Under the sway of blind passion they imagined themselves fitted for happiness in the closest and most exacting of all relations, and promised to love and cherish each other until death. But love cannot be given in payment of promise or delivered to fulfil a pledge, and in many cases those who were bound together found themselves unfitted by nature and training to live in harmony. Instead of the benefits that conjugal union should bring to life and character, there was discord and degradation of spirit. Society for its own protection forbade the easy dissolution of the galling bond, and from the enforced unions came offspring endowed with perversities of temper and physical, mental and moral imperfections that marred their whole lives beyond cure.

"This kind of hap-hazard and ill-assorted marriage is no longer known. Children of both sexes are brought up with an understanding of themselves and of each other, and of this, as well as of other relations in life, which prepares them to assume the duties and the delights of married existence, with assurance against the old risks of misery. Love is of course a matter of sentiment and is not without the glow of passion, but it is under the sway of wisdom. It almost always happens that when a young couple have such an affection for each other that they desire to live together and have families of their own, they have known each other so long and so well, and moreover, have been familiar with the lives and characters of so many others of their own age, that they are sure of their fitness for a permanent union and incur none of the old-time chances of wreck. Besides, they never fail to consult their friends and relatives who are older than themselves, and to be guided by their counsel. As no selfish or sordid object is ever sought, and as the sole desire is to reach the conclusion that will best assure the welfare and happiness of those concerned, it has long been a rare thing to have to mourn over a mistaken marriage or to consider questions of separation.

"This state of things in regard to the marriage relation, together with the care given to the birth as well as the training of children, has had a most potent effect upon the progress which this people has made within a few generations. The effect upon family life has been most elevating and strengthening. The affection between husband and wife grows day by day more complete; slight incongenialities disappear, until there is hardly more than a single self wherein the two lives pass in happy accord through death to an indissoluble union in the spirit life.

"In the old days of the turbulence of the passions and the waywardness of folly, it was customary to surround the union of man and wife with sanctions of religion and obligations of law. These are no longer necessary. Nothing but love can make such a union sacred and nothing else can make it enduring. Now there are no formalities or ceremonies attending marriage of which the State or Church takes any note. It is a personal and family affair, sanctified by love and made secure by the obligations of love and duty.

"No longer are children begotten in heedless disregard of the lives that are to await them, or born to reluctant parents, unfit or unable to give them proper support and training. The passions are in subjection to reason and every child is the offspring of deliberate purpose. The number of children in a family is determined by the wishes of parents and their ability to provide adequately for them, and the whole community is made up of happy families. The greatest misfortune, now very rare, is to be precluded by any circumstance from the joy and benefit of family life. These homes are often occupied by two or three generations of the same family living in the utmost concord.

"These houses that you see spreading with their flowery gardens and verdant lawns in ever-broadening circles about each city and finally scattering in rural habitations over the intervening country, are each the possession of its occupants. Those who are old enough do their share in the work of the community; they devote a portion of each day's time to studying and gathering wisdom, they have their hours given to rational pleasure, and they are at peace with each other and their neighbors.

"There are no barriers between home and home, and nothing is locked up or guarded by night or day. Honesty and universal good-will are an all-sufficient protection for person and property."

IX.

THE HIGHER MORALS AND RELIGION.

"But," I asked, "have these people no government and no laws?"

"There is little need of government or laws in such a state of society. Wickedness and folly make these necessary, and scarcely a vestige of those qualities remain, not enough to require a system of protection against them. The effect of the wonderful progress made by this people has not been to increase the functions of government, but to diminish them, until only a few of the simplest survive. Ages ago the necessity of dealing with crime and destitution disappeared. With the prevalence of general intelligence, universal honesty, and the desire to do right, even to sacrificing self-interest for the benefit of others, all need of complicated systems for the settlement of disputes and difficulties involving personal and property rights departed. When the ancient order of things, under which there were various nations, with diverse interests, gave way to a universal brotherhood, all necessity for regulating the relations of different countries was gone, and the era of armies and navies and conflicting national interests is recalled as a barbarism of the distant past.

"All industrial and commercial affairs go on smoothly under the regulation of a voluntary co-operation, which works effectually through every branch and in every field of effort, applying itself to the precise extent that it is required to accomplish the desired results. Where there can be absolute trust and confidence, and where suspicion of wrong is never entertained, the machinery of administration is amazingly simplified.

"Government, so far as it exists is

wholly local. Each of these great communities with its centre for mechanical production and commercial interchange, and its wide surroundings of rural and industrial life, forms a unit for all public purposes, and the communication between them, which is absolutely free, needs no public regulation. In each there are certains functions of general utility,—such as furnishing supplies of water, heat, light, and constructing and maintaining roads and other means of quick and constant communication,—in short, the regulation of all appliances of common use,—and these are subject to public control. It is the application of the co-operative principle to the whole community. Everything that is a concern of all the people, as distinguished from their personal affairs and the business and employments which they regulate among themselves by systems of voluntary co-operation, is conducted as a public function, and the administration of such matters is placed in the hands of men qualified by character and experience for the work.

"The choice of men for these public duties is by no means so difficult a matter as it might seem to be to one who has just come from a life where selfishness is still the ruling influence. No man seeks the honor or emolument of public office, for there is no greater reward of either kind attached to it than the same man would have in private station, and no one shirks the duty and responsibility if they are assigned to him by the general voice. By common consent it is only men of mature years and long experience who are selected for these public functions, and each is paid an equivalent of the income which he has to give up in order to devote his time to the public business.

"Every year, in each of these centre communities, one hundred men are chosen from the whole body of the people to constitute the Administrative Council for all public affairs. This body has the entire power of regulation and legislation, and through its own committees, or subdivisions, and through designated officials from its own members it performs all executive functions. The ability, experience, integrity and unselfish public spirit of these men, always assured by the popular choice, are an unquestioned guarantee of the most efficient, honest, and economical management. The Administrative Council once chosen for the year, the people leave the public business in its keeping with entire confidence.

"I have learned that this is the manner of electing the Council: In the great community which we are now overlooking yonder spacious structure of a single story, with the succession of arched roofs of glass, is the one public service building. It contains the Council Chamber and all necessary offices and bureaus and a great amphitheatre for popular gatherings. There is in this structure a polling room for receiving the votes of the people, which may be deposited in person or sent in by mail. At any time during what corresponds in our minds to the first ten months of the year, names may be sent in for the next council. They may be members of the existing council or not, and every citizen, signing his ballot, may in this way suggest such names as he pleases, not exceeding the number to be chosen. At the end of this nominating period a month is allowed for sifting from the ballots the three hundred candidates receiving the highest number of votes, if there are so many in all, and from these the final selection is made.

"For this purpose the polls are kept open during the last month of the year. Each citizen may vote for one or more of the designated three hundred candidates, as he pleases, within the limit of one hundred, but not give more than one vote for the same candidate, and the one hundred receiving the highest number are declared elected. As the record of voting is constantly kept during its progress the declaration is made at once upon the closing of the polls on the last day of the year.

"This seems at first cumbersome if not complicated, but there is so much intercourse and interchange of opinions and such universal honesty and singleness of purpose that there is no great number of candidates suggested in excess of the number required for the council. Before the end of the year there is a very general agreement upon the one hundred to be chosen. There is no secrecy about voting and no occasion for safeguards against any sort of dishonesty or fraud, the discovery of which would create amazement as great as would be produced by a case of insanity or the appearance of a pestilence.

"There is really less of public employment than you might suppose, as there is much voluntary service, which includes pretty much all the teaching and providing for the cultivation and entertainment of the people. The benefit is regarded as mutual, those that give deriving as much satisfaction as those that receive."

"But," I said, "a public fund, and hence some system of contribution or taxation, must be necessary for those public functions which are equally for the advantage of all, but nobody's individual interest to provide."

"Well, but to whom, think you, do this planet and its natural treasures and opportunities belong? To the people who have been placed upon it, do they not? Yet in the application of their labor and skill in turning the natural resources to account, different persons must occupy different areas and spaces, whether farms and gardens, mines and quarries, or sites for factories and warehouses. The values which they produce by applying their labor and skill fairly belong to themselves, but not the spaces which they have taken. These are part of the common heritage supplied by nature and its beneficent author.

"Whatever the value of mere occupation of space may be to the individual, he owes to the community, and to the community he pays it freely and gladly for the general benefit. The revenue from this source is ample for every public purpose, and furnishes the means for all the general appliances of convenience, comfort and enjoyment that are not supplied by private generosity, in which there is a constant emulation among those possessed of a superfluity. Where such a spirit prevails as is plainly dominant here, there is little need of rulers or of laws, and government in the sense with which we are familiar has been outgrown. All revenue for the common purposes of the people is derived from the virtual rental to individuals of that which is by right the common possession of the people, the land upon which God has placed them, and that revenue is gladly paid to the common treasury and is ample for all public needs. Hence no burden or restriction is put upon the production and interchange of the fruits of labor."

"But do the women," I asked, "take their share in all kinds of work?"

"Every being does the work that is adapted to his or her capabilities, no matter what that work may be. All distinctions are based on individual qualities and not on social divisions of any kind. There are no such divisions. There are duties and tasks for which women are specially fitted, and they naturally accept these, but no individual is under restraint or requirement of any kind. Woman has her place in the family to care for the young, to look after the household, the home and its surroundings, and there is her chief delight; but any of the work of the community that she may like to do is open to her. In the libraries and lecture-rooms and museums, men, women and children learn together, each pursuing the studies for which his taste fits him.

"Schools of the ancient sort with their disciplinary restraints and regulations do not exist. Despotism is no more necessary for children than for grown people.

In learning, as in everything else, there is liberty. All who know are teachers to any that desire to learn the things they know, and all are learners from any that may be in advance of themselves in any field of knowledge. There is, in fact, mutual helpfulness in all things. Of course all this is not left at hap-hazard; on the contrary there is the most perfect system. The schools are sedulously graded, so that there may be no waste of time or energy, and the rule of "the fittest" is the principle on which both teachers and pupils find their natural places—under guidance of directors chosen for the purpose. As all wish to learn, ancient questions of discipline are obsolete; it is rather like a well-ordered garden, where each plant is helped to grow according to its own nature and possibilities.

"The knowledge obtained is not perfect, for knowledge cannot be perfect short of infinity; but these people have thoroughly explored their globe and examined its treasures, whether buried in the soil and rocks or in the sea. Its composition and its natural laws they know with something approaching completeness of knowledge. Their apparatus and appliances for aiding in the acquisition of knowledge are far more effective than anything yet devised on our earth. They have studied the surrounding heavens with instruments of marvellous power and exquisite perfection, and long ago discarded the narrow notion natural to all undeveloped peoples that their world was the centre of the universe for which all the rest was made to minister, and themselves the only sentient beings in this infinity of worlds."

"I do not see any churches or temples of worship among these people," I said to my friend, as we passed unseen among the structures of one of their greatest cities.

"No," he replied, "there are no longer any costly fanes specially devoted to worship, and there is scarcely anything that can be called public worship. Ages ago these people attained a practical unanimity of opinion and of sentiment on matters of religion and moral conduct. They reached a degree of enlightenment that made it clear to them that there was but one standard of moral character and conduct, and that its observance was in every way conducive to the well-being and happiness of the individual and of the community. Much time in their schools, their homes and all their gathering places is still devoted to teaching and to learning in matters that relate simply to moral duty or pertain to the relations of men with each other.

"For a long time they maintained special organizations for this work of moral instruction and elevation, but they have now outgrown the need of them, and an all-pervading influence to the same end is kept up in all they do. It is a part of the normal social spirit that has become fully prevalent. These special organizations, now disused, sprang originally out of religious societies formed mainly for worship at a time when worship had many forms and phases of superstition. In the dark times, when views of the Creator and of the nature and destiny of his creatures were obscured in ignorance and credulity; when there was a constant struggle between the spiritual aspirations and moral tendencies of the inhabitants of this planet and the impulses and passions of their animal nature; when many of them still had natures that were distorted and beset with degrading inclinations; in short, before knowledge and experience had begotten that wisdom which has resulted in the mastery of right over wrong—then there were many forms of belief and manners of worship.

"These men as we may as well call them, in that remote age held different views of the Creator and of his relations and dealings with them, according to the degree of enlightenment which they could attain, and out of these grew systems of belief and methods of worship which were a help to them in their efforts at progress and the elevation of their race. The stimulus and restraint of a belief in a higher Power and of a humble and devout worship of that Power were necessary to their moral advancement. While they were in the darkness of ignorance and unreason this belief and this worship took various forms which were maintained by many organizations.

"With the growth of knowledge and the full development of reason they gradually came nearer to the truth and attained a clearer conception of the God of the universe and of his attributes, of their own nature and destiny, and of the relation their life held to the universal and eternal Life. With this advancement their many forms of belief melted into one universal faith, as the errors due to ignorance and superstition lost their hold and dropped away. Now they have but one religion of all-comprehensive simplicity and purity, and no formal worship.

"I do not mean by this that they are not devout, that they give no thought to things divine, or that they do not worship God. Neither do I mean that they have no associations based upon religious sentiment. They associate constantly, for all manner of common purposes, and the essential principle of their society is mutual helpfulness. It is a principle that pervades all their life, their industry, their business and their public work of every kind. For generations they maintained organizations to see that nobody suffered from sickness or misfortune where it could be helped, to see that the conditions of health and comfort and fair opportunities in life were provided for all, and the result was gradually to establish a social system in which all these things were fully cared for. They have associated together for a general diffusion of education, of knowledge and right views upon all matters affecting their welfare, that the whole stock of wisdom may be open equally to all and its benefit made as great as possible.

"There is nothing in which they have been more assiduous than the inculcation of sound and wholesome sentiments and principles of conduct, and they are not only not negligent of the spiritual side of their nature, but it has long been the subject of special study with them and they are careful of its training. Much of what was mysterious to us on earth, and to them in earlier times, and was vaguely regarded as supernatural and incomprehensible, they have brought within the domain of their knowledge, and they have established a clearer relationship with the unseen world than to us seemed possible. With a fuller understanding of the spiritual and divine their sympathies have been greatly developed on that side, and the sentiment of devotion and worship has been exalted and freed from the grossness and crudeness that characterized it at a stage of less enlightenment. This sentiment is cherished by proper exercise and cultivated by association; it is fostered in the young and in those in whom it appears to be naturally feeble, and yet all this is rather a part of the general life than a matter of special organization and formal effort. It is involved in the universal system of instruction and intercourse of the community.

"Worship of God and communion with the Spirit of the universe in the loftiest sense must be an affair of each individual soul, for which no special time or place is required. In the stage of advancement which this race has attained, religious worship needs no set forms and methods, and its outward expression is no longer a matter of publicity. The loftiest sentiments and purest emotions are appealed to and gratified in literature and the nobler arts, and in the many social and public gatherings of the people they seek the joy and stimulus of communion with each other in the highest aspirations of the soul as well as the loftiest themes of thought. But it is only in the privacy of his home or the secrecy of his own heart that the individual addresses himself to a communion with the Father of all life. In short, on this planet, religion has ceased to be a system, and has become the pervading spirit of the social order and of the daily life of the people.

"This is the result of long ages of advancement during which great teachers and leaders have successively arisen, pointing the way of elevation more and more clearly, and manifesting in their own lives the capabilities of the race. The ideal was thus made ever more clear and more accessible, until the mass of this people have well-nigh attained it for all the purposes of their mortal existence.

"This planet and its people have greatly interested me ever since I discovered them, because they remind me of the earth on which my days were passed before the great change, and seem to exemplify the perfected state toward which humanity is struggling there and which it may reach in the time to come."

While this discourse went on by means of that spiritual interchange of ideas that has no need of physical organs or senses, our party of visitants floated gently among the people and observed their ways of life, being often aware even of their thoughts and feelings. Some of them would at times pause in meditation, dimly conscious of our presence and plainly feeling its influence. We could by our own volition make it felt to various degrees according to the temperament or the mood of the persons affected. Our own intercourse with each other was that of a quick and constant intercommunion of thought and feeling, and my beloved wife seemed to be truly a part of myself.

As I contemplated the joyous existence of this happy race and the comparative perfection it had attained, it seemed almost as though the purpose of its physical life had been fulfilled. To my friend I said:

"You have told me that the inhabitants of this planet are now free from the diseases and ills of the flesh because they long ago ceased to propagate and perpetuate them, and because they have gained such a knowledge of the laws of nature and such skill and fidelity in observing them as to maintain in their habits and surroundings the conditions of perfect health. But in process of time they die. We see evidences of that."

"Surely they die," was the answer, "but rarely except from the natural decline and decay of the physical powers. They generally live a full century (or more, according to their larger measure of time), but at last the body is worn out and its functions cease. By that time the soul is fully ripe for the spirit-world and passes with joy to the abodes of the blest, while the body is laid away to dissolve into dust or be reduced to the elements by the quicker processes of nature. There is no dread of death, for all know that it is not a calamity. The function of the fleshly vesture is fulfilled; the soul is prepared to live without it, and puts it off most gladly.

"No one mourns for the death of friend or parent, knowing well that it is but a passage to a fuller life, and that the separation will not be long. There is no parade of grief, for there is no grief. No honors or attentions are paid to the cast-off body or its resting place, for the body is not the person nor the grave his dwelling. Why should the spot where the decaying chrysalis is put away be surrounded with emblems of remembrance, when the spirit of the loved has gone to the unseen life? The thoughts go with the soul into life and not with the body into dust and ashes.

"Every one here is prepared to die, for a character has been formed which will stand the test of the spiritual existence. Souls come up from this planet continually, far purer and stronger than those that come from our earth, save that a few great ones from that young and struggling world have, in spite of impediments and obstacles, risen to a grander stature than their fellows, and come into the spirit world fit for association with the highest. And this fuller stature is not one of mere intellectual power, for many a man has had that, and yet been a spiritual dwarf; it involves an intuitive perception of the mutual relation of spirit with spirit—man with his fellows and with the Father of all—and a habit of life in accordance with those relations. The simplest single earthly word you have to express the quality I mean is *love;* yet that must be largely, and not selfishly, interpreted.

"From all these worlds that revolve in space come trooping millions of spirits that God has breathed into being to people his universe. They have struggled through the embryo stage of their existence with varied experiences and enter upon 'the life indeed' with every degree of development. The eternal years are before them and the boundless opportunities of the universe."

As our spirit group lingered, hovering over that scene of active and happy life,

I exclaimed: "Here behold the blessed possibilities of the unhappy planet that I have left! If the people of the earth would learn the great lessons of truth and assimilate them into their lives, they might be even as the inhabitants of this happy sphere, one great brotherhood pervaded with peace and harmony.

"Here riches and poverty are unknown and both alike undesired, while on earth they are prolific sources of wrong and unhappiness. Here all take their share of toil, and necessary work is done without crushing any into suffering and misery with its tremendous burden. There is no ignorance and no crime, and hence the cost and cruelty of laws and government are unknown. Ingenuity, intellectual activity, and mutual consideration seem to have wrought for the people the conditions of a healthy life.

"Now there are on earth thousands of persons as well inclined to do right and live in harmony with the universe as this people, and if all could be brought to that condition, a millennium like that which we see here might be ushered in."

"Aye," was the response, "but it is better for the earth race, as for the individual man, to grow according to the law of its being and come up through conflicts and struggles to this condition. It will then be endowed with strength won by its own efforts.

"In ages long past this people, too, groped in darkness and grappled with each other in terrific conflicts, striving and groaning for the light. Then were there ignorance and sloth and crimes and laws, superstition and systems of religion, wealth and poverty, fights and wars and destruction and suffering and misery, but always there were souls serene and strong that rose above the conflict of discordant elements and saw the truth and the right in their simple purity. These never wearied from generation to generation in warring with the powers of darkness and striving to lead the people up from their bondage and degradation.

"Slowly the light gained upon the darkness. The teachers wrought patiently through the discouraging eras and wisdom gained ground. Laws and systems of faith, which were as props to secure what had been gained and give footholds for further advances, became simpler and fewer as man grew wiser and stronger, until at last the hosts of the right prevailed and the enemies of peace were overthrown. The edifice of the race's redemption on this bright planet was slowly and painfully reared by his own efforts, working more and more in harmony with the laws of the universe and of the Divine Spirit that pervades it.

"The earth which we have left is in the midst of its struggles now, and the leaders and champions of right feel that their work is not in vain. They are redeeming their race through constant crucifixions, and by the beneficent laws of compensation they are gaining from their labors and sufferings the power which is the real object of mortal life."

X.

SPIRIT RELATIONSHIP AND ACHIEVEMENT.

Now we turned from this happy sphere and glided back through the heavenly spaces. Everywhere about us as we went were spirits of the immortals, some bound on distant missions, others gathered together in converse and communion, families and friends, great ones and humble, all intent upon the joyful activity of the eternal life.

Their surroundings, discernible by the disembodied soul, were fraught with glories and beauties which to physical sense would be imperceptible and to those dependent upon physical senses must be incomprehensible. To picture them to the minds of mortals, I should speak of grottoes and retreats where loveliness of form and color were combined in perfect harmony, pervaded with all the charms of sound and odor that can delight the soul; of quiet groves, of lovely gardens, cool fountains, inviting slopes and refreshing shades, of gorgeous structures in the sublime ether, the grand architecture of nature in the free heavens, gleaming with hues brighter and more varied than light can furnish to human vision, and wrought with a perfection no artist or architect ever conceived in his most exalted dreams.

By such imagery alone can the mind of man gain some faint notion of the spiritual abodes; and yet their beauties are not material, are not beauties of form and color and are not filled with sounds and odors. Still, they are of a nature that gives to the disembodied spirit a far more perfect and exalted joy than could be conveyed by the senses of the flesh in their most exquisite state.

Through these scenes in their myriad forms we passed till we reached a quiet retreat in which seemed to be united everything that could delight the soul, and there with ineffable joy we reposed in what I may call our own home. My soul and my soul's beloved wife mingled in a manner that gave supernal joy, far more ecstatic than could be derived from any communion of spirits hampered in the body. Then did I feel that one moment of this joy that was to be eternal was compensation for all the sufferings of my mortal existence.

Reposing in this celestial home we remained for a time in a restful revery, like a dream of bliss. Then came again my desire to learn more of the new life.

"Ah!" I said, "our earthly hopes of reunion and of blessedness with those we loved were not unsubstantial dreams. Here we are united in the eternal home with unending years before us. The happiness of the earthly life was but a beginning, the interruptions of death were momentary. This is the real life and the ties formed there hold us here forever."

"Yes, it is so," returned my friend, "and yet the earthly beginning of these ties of family was not always right, and wrong cannot be perpetuated, Here there is truly no marriage, no carnal relationship, and all association is the result of natural attraction. Mortals on earth are wont to call marriage 'sacred, divine'; but it is and ever was a device of man—a necessary safeguard in an imperfect state of society—while love alone is sacred.

"Marriage is far from being a holy institution in itself. Persons unfitted to enjoy each other's society, unfitted to promote each other's growth and development, unfitted to aid in ameliorating the race, assume with haste and folly a union which human laws force them to hold through a life perchance of hatred and unhappiness.

"No divine law compels such incongruous and wretched unions to continue here. Love is indeed divine, and where that exists and brings souls together while yet in the body, their communion is sweet, their influence upon each other is beneficent, they have offspring of still more gracious aspect and character than themselves. Such spirits will continue in their relations of love in the life eternal, —but that is only because they are relations of love, and not because they existed on earth or were in conformity with human laws.

"Thousands of unions on earth are sources of misery. When at last death effects a release which human society would not—perhaps cannot—countenance, then there is freedom at last. Every hated alliance is broken and there is no longer subjection of the will where affection is not. Every soul seeks communion with those that are the natural and satisfying objects of its love.

"Vast and varied are the relationships of this life, and every soul is involved in its destiny with all others, but the intimacy of association is in exact proportion to the natural congeniality of the spirits. No matter what former relations or ties may have existed under the restraints of human laws and the necessities of human society, here freedom is perfect and universal. Each spirit seeks out for its love those that understand itself and have an attraction for it, and cleaves to none other. There is the most intimate communion where this attraction is strongest, and affection grows wherever characters are adapted to excite it in each other.

"A soul let loose in the heavens will soon find out its companions and always join its own company. Those for whom it has most love, it may have been separated from through most of its former existence, and those that it lived with may be the ones in whom it finds no reciprocal attraction.

"Many souls are united after long estrangement and cruel separation, and marriage may be what separated them. Families may, indeed, be separated in heaven, but only when they are not fitted to be together.

"Many a wife will leave a husband she ought never to have had and will find her supreme joy with one whom she can really love; aye, with thousands whom she loves—if you will dissociate that word from its lower misuses, and take its nobler, truer meaning. Husbands that were, if they loved not their wives, cleave to them no longer but seek the companionship of those whom they do love. In short, the human relations continue just so far as they were relations of love, and no farther; and where love is, there will the demonstrations of love abound.

"There is no conflict, and no jealousy; for where freedom is perfect jealousy cannot exist. Our associations are manifold, and love of one does not exclude love of another. Certain necessities and purposes of the mortal existence created exclusiveness and restraints, but here there are none. Those necessities and purposes no longer have force, and the freedom of love is perfect.

"The consummation of love in communion and interchange of thought and feeling has nothing in it of carnal limitations. Wives and husbands, children and parents, brothers and friends, whose relationships sprang from love, find themselves bound together here with an affection more exalted and in a communion more perfect; but those relationships that were forced and unnatural are abandoned and forgotten. There is indeed no marriage or giving in marriage, no families defined by law or kept together by restraint, but perfect freedom, perfect harmony and perfect bliss in communion of spirits.

"The harmony of disembodied souls is ever increasing. Many come here whose character is likely to produce discord, but they find around them benign influences and every encouragement and assistance to develop their better powers and capacities. Growth and development are characteristics of this life as of that on earth. Spirits find themselves here oftentimes but little developed, on account of the untoward circumstances of their earthly experience, and such have their lives to begin almost anew. Others have been crippled and distorted and have a thousand stubborn faults to correct."

"But," I said with surprise, "do the bad, the wicked, the vicious, the criminal, enjoy the same advantages as the good and virtuous?"

"Ah!" said the spirit with a kind of angelic sadness, "who shall judge and punish the wicked? An all-wise Creator has brought the human race into being and placed it on yonder little planet, with all its powers, its capabilities and its tendencies, to grow up through struggle and conflict, through error and wrong, into the strength and purity of a perfected state.

"Some with happy endowments and favoring circumstances may attain a goodly growth during the lifetime of the body, but the growth of the race as a whole is the process of many generations. Meantime thousands are constantly falling in the struggle and are trodden under foot; thousands wander far astray; and of the millions that are continually perishing from the face of the earth few have fairly got started on their life. The laws most favorable to the whole in the long process of growth, necessitate the crushing down of many for the time being; and who shall condemn them for their misfortune?

"It is the lot of many a soul to receive in the conception and gestation of the bodily organism, tendencies which, with a feeble will and no encouragement, it cannot overcome and can but weakly resist. It is blind as to its own nature and destiny, and no one imparts light and knowledge to it. It violates continually the laws of bodily and spiritual well-being and receives continually the penalty that follows as an inevitable consequence. It was planted in a bad soil with conditions unfavorable to healthy growth, and becomes wild, rank and noisome.

"Another soul is introduced to life through a more wholesome medium and begins with tendencies toward a healthy development and circumstances which favor and encourage it. It becomes vigorous, symmetrical and pure.

"There is struggle and effort such as the person is capable of in both cases; in one success, in the other almost total failure. The merit and the blame in the eye of the All-wise differ but little in the two cases. Both souls leave the body. One finds itself fitted for association with the pure and good, the wise and great of the race, and ready for the activities and the renewed and vigorous growth of the celestial life. This is compensation enough for sufferings and drawbacks such as he has had. The other sees at last the great destiny of being, but finds itself far from its attainment, unfitted for its joys, almost an outcast from the celestial hosts, not because they cast it out, but because the character it brings does not fit it for their company. Is not this sufficient punishment, if punishment is deserved? Should not this poor soul's forlorn condition excite pity and compassion rather than resentment and wrath?

"Every spirit that has passed from the body and its limitations and entanglements has enough left of the instinct of growth and the yearning for perfection to begin with new hope, for without hope nothing can be attained.

"These unhappy ones are taken from the wilderness in which they got continually lost; they are freed from the passions and appetites pertaining to the flesh, which drove them into pits and sloughs; they find that the spirits of the just and good do not look on them with disdain but with pity and love, and are ready to give them aid and encouragement. So the poor dwarfed, distorted cripples soon come into relations of sympathy with happier spirits and begin to learn the great lessons of life. They labor with an eagerness which those can hardly show who have not been through the darkness that they have passed, and they feel a joy more keen for the misery they have endured.

"Their moral sufferings are gradually transmuted into sinews of strength and they make their way up among the wise and good, growing in knowledge, in power and in purity, and feeling a pleasure in them which former privations intensify. Surely they have compensation and not cruel punishment for the disadvantages of their earthly existence.

"Children come here with little or no earthly experience. This is a disadvantage, but it has its compensation, also, for they have few wrong tendencies to correct and no evil habits to remedy. They are taken in charge by loving teachers who train them tenderly in the knowledge and grace which are the objects of life. In this sphere of development the stages reached are infinitely varied, but every person is striving on toward perfection, which can be attained only in eternity. The knowledge to be acquired is infinite, the faculties to be developed have no strict limitation, and only an eternity can complete the process of growth to perfection.

"Every condition of spiritual character comes here from the earth and from the other worlds, and each has something to impart to the others. The qualities and experiences of all the individuals have their effect in forming the character of the whole. Some have been here for what on earth would be regarded as long ages, but even with their enlarged powers and the greater facilities of the spirit world, they have scarcely begun upon the infinite resources of life. There are no false standards of judgment, but every soul speedily finds the place to which it is entitled by the qualities it brings with it or which it attains.

"Many that were high and mighty in the earthly life are humbled when they find for the first time what they really are, and are forced to take their place below the peasant and the slave who strove after spiritual power and not after wealth and high station, which are no measure of true greatness of soul. Many come up through poverty and hardship, through toil and struggle, and find themselves ready to take up the tasks of this life far in advance of some to whom they had looked up, regarding them not only as great and powerful but as good and saintly beyond their own hopes."

"But the truly great ones of earth," I asked, "where are they? The saints and sages, the poets and philosophers, those who conquered the hearts of men by the might of intellect, surely they retain their pre-eminence!"

"Yes, but man yof them had lessons to learn which the obscure had acquired before them. Those were not alone the really great, even in intellect, who were known as such; many an unknown and unambitious thinker was the peer of those who gained the widest repute, while those who lived in the mouths of men had unnoted weaknesses which belittled them. Here all are measured by an absolute standard, and there is no place for pretension. Every soul passes for what it is.

"Still, those powers which any possess

in a higher degree than others they exercise in the pursuit of their favorite investigations and labors. The unlimited fields of truth are before them and their powers and facilities, actual or to be attained, are as limitless. Each can follow his chosen pursuit. One studies the material elements of the universe, their qualities, operations and laws, while another is engaged in learning of spiritual things; and as each advances in the conquest of truth, he becomes a teacher of others and the advancement of all is promoted.

"The man of science makes calculations vaster than the universe of his mortal conception, penetrates mysteries which had hitherto seemed forever shut against him, and takes all knowledge for his province with hope of bringing it to perfect subjection in the endless time. The philosopher thinks with untrammelled intellectual power and soars on forever, broadening and strengthening his grasp upon abstract truth, and ever approaching but never reaching a perfect knowledge of God and His purposes and meaning, for even here and to us the divine being is an eternal mystery.

"On earth our conception of God had but a glimmer of truth. Now we know Him as the all pervading spirit of the universe that manifests His activity in every operation of nature throughout the numberless worlds, contains us all within His own being, and is everywhere an intelligence and a power, full and perfect. We perceive His presence by the spiritual intuition, as we perceive that of each other; we commune with Him as the finite may with the infinite, and yet we cannot comprehend His vastness in wisdom, in power and in love, and we only draw nearer and nearer to a perfect comprehension as in the long epochs of eternity we acquire knowledge more and more complete of His creation, of the operations of His might, of the objects of His care and His perfect methods in dealing with them.

"As our love for each other grows in intensity and expands so as to take in more of our fellow beings, we begin to comprehend more of His infinite love; and we approach more nearly to it, the more fully we love all the beings and all the things that He has made, for His love in its infinite perfection embraces all with equal warmth.

"On earth we were ever striving to imitate in our puny way the works of God. Our efforts to comprehend His creation and His being were but strivings toward what He is. Artists rejoiced in success only as they could copy Him in conception and in achievement, and they were great only as they approached God. The musician endeavored to produce sounds that should be some faint echo of His eternal harmonies. The poet tried to grasp His thought and feeling, and body it forth in language that should make others thrill in response to its beauty and wisdom.

"Here it is the same in a higher degree. All are striving to reach God through His works. Those who are learning to comprehend Him and growing in His likeness are fulfilling their destiny. Here, too, are poets and musicians, and artists, seeking finer harmonies, and subtler beauties, and giving them voice and form in such manner that other spirits comprehending them are exalted and purified. All are striving in their several ways to learn what God has done, and trying to do something Godlike. Thus through the ages of eternity, their growth is toward God.

"The faculties of the disembodied soul find constant employment, and this is a busy life; but there are periods of repose. Amid the glories of heaven the soul may settle into a blissful quietude, drinking in, as it were, in a revery or an exalted dream, the beauties and harmonies that surround him. He may hold the active powers in suspense and float in joyous idleness."

As my friend ceased his discourse, I remained for a time in such serene repose as he had just described. Then my mind began to wander back to earth, and I thought of the possibility of sometime making visits there, as we had visited the far-off planet and its happy race. It seemed to me that I might find satisfaction in observing the progress of the human race toward a higher state, though there was no person left behind toward whom I had any yearning.

With this thought I once more questioned my friend. "There was among us on earth," I said, "a cherished notion that the spirits of the departed were wont to return and watch over the living, attending them in their daily walks, soothing them in sorrow and suffering, and hovering about them to their journey's end, ready to receive them at the moment of death and take them to the abodes of happiness."

"Yes, but the thought was born of our weakness and our selfishness. Doubtless spirits have the power to visit the earth, as they may visit any spot in all the vast universe, and they may linger in familiar places and watch those still in the flesh, but would it be well for them to do so constantly? Those living on earth are undergoing the needed discipline of early growth, appointed to them by the Creator under his unchanging laws. We cannot relieve them from any part of the burden or the hardship, and would not if we could, for we trust God's wisdom and know that what is allotted to them is the best.

"The duration of the earthly struggle is brief, and those to whom it is hardest will find the after life all the richer. Besides, this is a life of activity and of duty, and there are more desirable things to do than lingering near those whom we cannot help and can hardly comfort or encourage. We do indeed return at times and find satisfaction in re-visiting familiar scenes, and we take an interest in the circumstances and achievements of those we know. In cases of peculiar hardship or extreme sorrow we may be drawn to linger for a time about them and make our presence felt, soothing the feelings of suffering ones with the consciousness that we are near.

"Oftentimes have your beloved wife and sister and I been near you in your days of loneliness, but nothing that we could do would relieve it, and we knew that it was wholesome for the soul, and the recompense was to come. We never made our presence known, and though you may often have thought of us as hovering about you, you never felt any certainty of our presence."

"It is possible, then," I said, "for the disembodied spirit to make its presence known to the living and perhaps to communicate with them!"

"Undoubtedly it is possible. One mind, while still in the body, may exert an influence over another. When it is freed from the limitations of the physical organism, it may do this still more completely. Sometimes it will do so unconsciously to the subject and for a beneficent purpose, directing one's course in dark times and uncertain places. Sometimes a person peculiarly constituted or in an abnormal condition may be affected by this influence to a remarkable degree, with results that are mysterious to those who do not understand the source and nature of the influence. But it is better for those still in the earthly life to attend to the duties of that life and leave the secrets of the other till admitted to them in the natural course of things. If the life of the present is wisely conducted the life of the future is always safe.

"Besides, efforts to fathom by direct communication those mysteries that are wisely shut from the view of mortals in order that the discipline of the preliminary life may be more complete, are apt to produce unwholesome delusions and misleading fancies. The craving for such revelations becomes morbid and absorbing; it blinds the judgment and displaces real faith with gross credulity, and leads to deception and to perversion of the natural sentiments. When the brain or nervous system is in a state of unnatural excitement, the mind becomes subject to hallucinations. It may see visions and hold conversations purely imaginary, which seem to it so real that it has full faith in their reality.

"Persons in this morbid state think they see the forms of the departed as they knew them on earth, with the same bodily lineaments and even the familiar dress, when the reasoning mind knows that the bodily features are undistinguishable dust, the clothing surely can have no spiritual existence, and the soul is a thing not to be seen with the material eye. Yet many people who are reasonable on all subjects that concern their actual life, become superstitious and irrational when dealing with matters that concern death and that portion of life which is beyond.

"Spirits while still in the body have duties and activities pertaining to their mortal state and the early growth of their faculties. The purposes of their earthly existence will be best fulfilled if they attend to that life and the training of the soul for a higher state of being. This will not preclude a salutary contemplation of the destiny appointed for man, as revealed in his nature and his experience, and foreshadowed by the deeper intuitions of his soul and the exalted faith of those whose spirits are most in harmony with the all-pervading spirit in which we have our existence. Life in the body has a sympathetic contact with the life that is above and around it, and may draw inspiration from it that is uplifting and purifying, but not through efforts at a personal communion which the limitations of the bodily senses make impossible.

"Here the same beings that have passed through the earthly experience enter upon a new phase of the same life, and must devote themselves to its duties, looking forward and not backward, advancing through higher and higher stages of development, approximating more and more toward perfection of knowledge and of power, increasing by using these for the benefit of others, and assuming more and more the divine character throughout the æons."

XI.

SNATCHED FROM THE HEAVENLY LIFE.

Here then was I, entered upon the life eternal, or rather upon the second stage of it, for the life on earth was the beginning of the life eternal. Life once begun is immortal, and the dissolution of the body, which was necessary to the chrysalis state of being, is but an incident in its course. It involves a mighty change of conditions and circumstances but it is no interruption to the life of the soul or transformation of its character.

On this stage of life was I fairly entered, and in the ambrosial bowers and retreats of the celestial world I tasted ecstatic bliss with those whom I had loved on earth. No new love now conceived could ever supersede that which was begun amid the trials of the earthly state, for that love was complete.

I passed celestial hours with my wife and the little one who had never known aught of the troubles of earth, but was growing with unsullied purity in the atmosphere of heaven; with my parents, my sister, and the friend that had come before, whom now I felt to be in advance of me and capable more than ever of teaching and guiding me.

Not alone with these did I hold communion, but I enjoyed the society of the great and good of all ages, now purer and greater than ever before, but free from all assumption that they were higher or better than the least of God's creatures. In the converse of the wise and good I shared with rapture, and laid hold upon truths and exalted thoughts that my mind had never grasped before.

In this company were not alone those who were known as saints and sages in the mundane life,—poets, philosophers, scholars, martyrs and heroes, men and women of exalted souls and mighty thought from all parts of the world,— those called heathen as well as those known as Christian; but there were also those who had dwelt in obscurity even among their own people, whose lot was humble and whose most intimate associates had hardly known the great qualities they possessed. In that celestial society the pure, the strong, and the great, though on earth they may have been poor and despised, were accepted among their peers and became teachers of the great ones of the earth.

Among the rest was the One Jesus, he who had so thoroughly begun the heavenly life on earth, passing through the trials and sorrows of human existence without a stain. Exalted, beloved, sought on all sides, he was still meekest and lowliest among spirits, still as ever the Teacher, the Comforter, and the Revealer of great truths of God, which others had not yet learned. Still he taught that he was the son of God and all mankind were his brethren, that the human was ever divine, that the labor of the soul was to attain more and more to the stature of the Infinite by emulating His love and care for others. Highest in station, he had the highest bliss—of seeing the fruition of his life and love.

Yet in this goodly company to which I felt full assurance of free admission, in the sweet converse of friends and family, there was ever upon me an attraction, incomprehensible but irresistible, drawing me back toward the scenes of my mortal experience.

Why should I give a thought to that life, now gone and seemingly far away in the vague past, in the very beginning of the world and contemporary with the patriarchs and prophets? It seemed to me comparatively so small and mean that I wondered that I was ever enamored of it and had looked upon the coming of death with dread. Why should I think for a moment of leaving the new life with its labors and joys just opened to me?

The new attractions were strong and most sweet; and yet there was a tugging at my being, which in spite of myself would drag me back toward earth. Why, I knew not, and I struggled to resist it. I did not make it known to any, for I thought I could overcome it and it would pass away, and, strange as it may seem, my beloved ones were all unconscious of my struggle. At a fatal moment my power of resistance seemed to give way. The glories with which I was surrounded began to fade, the feeling of exaltation and of perfect freedom grew numb and vague, and I was aware that some power against which I was helpless was tearing me from this glorious life and carrying me back to earth.

The splendid scenes of that heavenly sphere slipped from my spiritual consciousness; the presence of my friends and of my celestial environment was gone as in the fitful changes of a dream, and now I seemed to be sweeping through the universe with the speed of light,—through the celestial spaces, past the rolling stars and the revolving systems. Anon I caught sight of our solar worlds. The sun, flaming and surrounded with surging clouds of fire, was marching on his appointed course, holding the planets with the strong lines of attraction as they spun in their circuits around him.

I saw the cold and distant orb of Neptune, Jupiter with his glowing belts, and Saturn hung in his flaming circles. Swiftly I entered the field in which these worlds circled in their appointed lines, glided past the moon with one side cold and torpid, the other shining and luminous, and all wild and desolate.

Then, the green earth grew in the blue space, till seas and continents were visible and mountains and valleys began to wrinkle its radiant brow. The cities and works of man appeared to view, and I plunged, as it were, into the very earth, with an uncontrollable impetus, and was in darkness and oblivion.

The racking pains, the unspeakable tortures with which I rose from that gulf, no human tongue can tell. First there was a glimmer of consciousness that went out in torment, and came again a little stronger. Presently I was aware of human forms gliding about me and ministering as to a sick person. Suddenly the sad fact forced itself on my enfeebled mind that I was back in that bruised and disfigured body, and must live on earth again. Fervently I prayed to be released, but the vital flame was rekindled in my poor body, and my infatuated fellow beings, instead of kindly quenching it, did all in their power to foster it into vigor.

I turned from the light and tried to bury myself in oblivion again. I rebelled against the well-meant ministrations of the living, and longed for death, not because my bodily sufferings were intolerable, but because I blessed death for its own sake and yearned to go back through it to the blissful life from which I had been snatched.

I need not tell the story of my mortal

sufferings, the tedious process of recovering bodily health and strength. It will suffice to reveal, what I had to learn from others, that for three days I had been as one among the dead. My body was terribly bruised and burned and, it was thought, internally injured. When taken from the wreck of the railroad train I was supposed to be already dead, but a certain flush and a quivering of the flesh made the doctors doubt.

In a rude farm-house I was laid, and every appliance was used to call me back to life. My burns were painted over to keep off the corrupting air, and my cuts and bruises bandaged, and yet corruption threatened and a sickening odor made my care a burden to the kind-hearted strangers. Restoratives were constantly used, although but the vaguest signs of life could be evoked.

On the third day the task of resuscitation was given up as hopeless, and the doctors pronounced me dead. I was unknown to those who attended me, and nothing on my person gave any clew to my home or friends, and so they had begun to make preparations to bury me on that green ridge in Vermont where the railroad accident had thrown me.

Scarcely had these preparations begun when a spasmodic motion and a flutter of the heart showed that life was still there, and the efforts at restoration were renewed. These, and the feeble force of vitality still in the body, together with the will of God, had drawn my soul back from the sweet heavens and the glorious life there and imprisoned it again in the mortal frame. I revived.

I was finally taken to friends whom I could still recall; and in the course of tedious months I could walk forth again.

Since that time I have been as a lonely exile, far away from his home. Others may say it is a delusion and a dream, but I know that my soul was for those three days parted from the body, and that I had a taste of the immortal life.

I walk among men, but no more am of

them. All their affairs seem to me petty and trivial. What they value most, I value least of all; and my thoughts are ever with the blessed beings in the great heavens, and dwelling on mysteries yet unfathomed.

I have never spoken of this experience to mortal man, for I know that it is impossible for men to comprehend or believe it. They would regard me as a lunatic and treat me accordingly. So I have kept my secret; and tried to bide my time to return to the life from which I was torn away when hardly past the threshold.

In pondering the mystery of my return through the portals of death, it has occurred to me that there was a divine purpose in it. There was need of a new revelation regarding the life and destiny of the human soul, and I was chosen to make it.

Humbly, meekly, I have adopted this interpretation of the mystery and tried simply to tell the world my experience, wherein, if anywhere, lies the revelation. I do not wish to be known to my fellow men, and desire that the identity of him who went through the gateway of death to the life beyond and returned against his will, shall be a secret. And that I may be speedily removed from a life in which I now account my mission fulfilled, to the life I know to be so much higher and better, is my constant prayer.

[The foregoing narrative constituted the bulk of the manuscript which the mysterious Mr. Jameson placed in the hands of the editor of this volume. Whether the experience which he professed to have had while apparently unconscious from the injuries received in a railroad accident, was real or imaginary, is not for the present writer to judge. That he believed it to be real, there is no reason to doubt.

Accompanying the narrative, but separate from it, was an essay, evidently intended as a statement of opinions and conclusions founded on the remarkable experience related. Probably it was written before the narrative, and originally meant to stand alone as an expression of the writer's views, without any explanation of the experience from which they were derived. There was, however, no prefatory explanation and the editor does not feel entitled to supply the omission of the author. He simply regards the paper as part of the "revelation" entrusted to him, and submits it with the rest to such judgment as it may invite.

It follows this.]

XII.

MAN'S REVELATION TO MAN.

Of the long period between the development of the race of man from its ancestry of brutes and the dawn of history at which it began to set up enduring and intelligible monuments, we know nothing save by scientific inference. The knowledge to be derived from the oldest surviving monuments and the first imperfect records has still to be largely supplied by inferences drawn from later history. It is the light of modern study and recent reasoning, cast over the past, that illumines that far-off dawn sufficiently to give meaning to its broken and defaced tablets, and to bring out the story which its confused and patched-up records contain.

All human history is a revelation of

man to man, and since the spiritual instinct began to work in the offspring of generations of brutes it has sought expression in ways and forms that have been called religion. These ways and forms have varied with the characteristics impressed upon the peoples among which they have appeared, by the circumstances of their origin and experience. Men of the clearest insight and loftiest conceptions have built up and modified religions, and thereby became prophets and priests. They have formed conceptions of a Deity behind things visible and behind the life of man. They have spoken for their God and been accepted as His interpreters.

There has been evermore a struggle to understand this earthly life and to guide its course to the highest good. There have also been yearnings for a life beyond this brief and troubled span, and various dreams of the soul's final destiny. Men who have risen above the spiritual level of their time and presented loftier views of the human and divine have seemed to their generation to make revelations from on high.

The notion of direct Divine revelation, by means of miraculous manifestations, has sprung from the inability of common men to comprehend the sources of the wisdom of seers and prophets. God works always and everywhere throughout his creation. Everything—whether material or spiritual—is a revelation of Him, and that revelation grows clearer as the soul increases in power and comprehension. External manifestations of His power and will through fire and whirlwind are not the methods of divine revelation and never were, but, as the old Hebrew prophet tells us, it is in "the still small voice" that speaks only in the consciousness of such human spirits as can hear it. When the more violent and awful phenomena of nature were not understood, it was natural to attribute them to the immediate presence and working of deity, and to connect with them the oracles of God.

In rude times the great minds among the people were wont to represent their thoughts and teachings as direct revelations from God, and even themselves regarded them as such. The manner in which these revelations had been communicated to them was surrounded with mystery to make them the more impressive and effective, and their mystery was exaggerated and amplified by those who put them on record, until men came to regard them not only as sacred but of literally divine origin. The rude devices of a primitive age to impress a superstitious people with awe and to hold them in restraint have been long after regarded as holy agencies through which God Himself has made known His will.

From age to age new ideas were taught among the same people, or another people springing up with different surroundings and a different experience had new conceptions of life and of human destiny, and a new religion was built up or the old one modified. The religion of a period or of a race has always been the expression more or less perfect of man's desires and longings, and of the best means he could devise for their satisfaction. It has been the outgrowth of the people's minds, the people's experience, and what they have learned of the life and experience that preceded them.

Nothing that has been called revelation has a divine perfection or a divine origin, except as the ultimate origin of everything is divine; and those older teachings and philosophies which men are wont to revere as sacred, are farther from truth and less sacred than the conceptions of later days.

Man's religion in its latest form, grounded on his highest knowledge, illumined by his clearest reason, inspired by his loftiest conceptions, is nearest the everlasting truth, and his best revelation is the last. He can have no revelation except of his own making. He began it with the first groping of the intellect, the first germ of the moral sense, the first flicker of the aspiring spirit. When it is finished his destiny will be complete.

What is this Holy Bible which men call the Word of God?

Consider the universe of rolling worlds inhabited by the creatures of the animating power that fills it, and think of its development through æons from the primeval chaos! On its myriad spheres are various forms and stages of life, and many degrees of growth toward the perfection which is the ultimate object of creative power. Consider the infinite spaces, already peopled with souls that have had their start in life upon those many spheres, and destined to be the eternal home of the spiritual offspring of God, when there shall be no further use for the material part of the universe! On one small planet amid these myriads, is this race of ours, struggling and contending in the early stages of moral and spiritual development, but with brightening hopes for each new generation.

The race of man knows little of its actual

origin upon the planet which it inhabits and less of the origin of the planet itself, but it has an imperfect record of the doings and achievements of the various branches of which it is composed. It can trace its own progress from the darkness of barbarism to the comparatively clear light that it is now attaining. Its students can see how, at some time and among some peculiarly endowed people the artistic sense grew to a high development and left its heritage; how at another stage and in another place there was a development of the organizing and instituting power, and the secret of regulating and governing was in part disclosed, to be more fully revealed by experience and growth; and all through human history is visible the growing recognition of moral principles by which conduct must be regulated in order that the race may survive and advance toward perfection.

When means of expression and communication were found, there came the written words through which the needs, the aspirations, the thoughts and imaginings of men found vent, and literature became the great agency of progress.

The universe is full of God's language. The man of science that ascertains a truth, reveals the word of God far more truly than the oracles of the ancient peoples of the world.

The Bible contains in its oldest part the writings of the earliest people whose history we know with any fulness, and the religion which we have been taught to revere, sprang out of the religion of that people. Hence it is that such a special sacredness has been attached to that mass of ancient literature. Much of it no doubt is sacred, for all truth is sacred and every good precept is holy, wherever it may be found; but the view which so many still take of those old writings is mainly due to the survival of ignorance and superstition.

As we look back over the progress of the human race, do we not see how after many glimmerings and gropings, the artistic sense in man, the love of the beautiful and refined, the genial amenities and humanities of life, and the spirit of philosophic inquiry, received a wonderful impulse and development in the little land of Greece? A people grew up there with a genius for those factors in human progress. Do we not find a little later another people in a neighboring land with a genius for aggressive force and conquest, for organization and law, for government and rule? These two peoples made their contributions to what we have been wont to call civilization, and the heritage passed to later times in the results of their history and in their literature.

More important than the artistic sense, and the instinct for refinement, more essential to permanent progress than the sense of power and the instinct for orderly rule, was the moral sense, inciting mankind to right conduct toward each other, and the recognition of obligation to a power above themselves.

This sense of duty was implanted in the human race with its other qualities, and along with those it struggled for the mastery; but like the peculiar aptitude of the Greek and of the Roman to teach the world in their great departments of advancement, so also a special genius for moral and spiritual development sprang up among the nomadic tribes of Arabia, and worked itself out in the Jewish religion and the Hebrew polity.

The half-mythical ancestor of Israel, the Chaldæan chief Abraham, the first to substitute the slaughter of animals for human sacrifices among his people, and to do away with the grosser rites of the worship of those dark times, gave to man the earliest exalted conception of a deity. Involved in the obscurity of myth, crudely reduced to matter-of-fact statement by prosaic writers, whatever personality was behind the august title of Abraham stood for a great moral and religious genius. From the gods of his pagan ancestors and kindred he chose for the worship of his tribe the Most High, the invisible creator of all gods and the father of men. But more than that, in paternal and patriarchal relation to his people, he conceived a lofty idea of purity in domestic and social life and of justice and integrity in the dealings of men. From such conceptions he clothed his God with the mystic attributes of justice, love and mercy, mingled with those of awful power proper to a mighty ruler. So far as we can discover in the mists of that far-off dawn of human history, Abraham, or the genius for which that name has stood for ages, was the first to inculcate submission and fidelity to the will of a higher power as a means of progress and elevation for mankind.

Under the impulse of this great conception the tribal and local deities of the ancestors of Israel, which superstition had created among them as among all primitive peoples, took a single personification, and men began to look up to one God. At first he was the God of the tribe, of a single people, jealous of all other gods; then he was the sovereign and ruler of the nation that sprang from that people; and finally, as the nation came to struggle for existence with other nations, it magnified its God into the creator of the earth and its destined ruler, after the subjugation of all other peoples to the sway of the chosen of Jehovah. The conception of God has gone through as remarkable an evolution as any other conception of the human mind, and the theocratic system of the ancient Hebrews did much for its development.

But it is impossible to identify the Jehovah of Israel with the conception of deity that must be derived from the knowledge that the human race has acquired in later ages. The Hebrews had their men of purely human genius as well as other ancient peoples, and one of these was that leader and law-giver who rescued them from Egyptian slavery and restored them to the land which they regarded as their heritage, where they built up a nation through many struggles and contests. Moses gained and maintained his ascendancy for the great work he had to do by appealing to the people's reverence for the God of Abraham, and by developing and elevating their conception of that deity. Instead of assuming to be a leader and a law-giver himself, he invested Jehovah with those functions and made him the sovereign. That was not only a stroke of political genius, but it marked a great advance in the people's conception of their God. It was natural that this unseen ruler should have the characteristics of an Oriental despot. At first he had even to be cruel and ruthless, vengeful and jealous, bloodthirsty and terrible, for the people could not be ruled without severity. Their God must be feared. He was terrible in his anger and fierce in his punishments, and he thundered his commands on the mountain tops and his threats in the tempest.

The worship of Jehovah by bloody sacrifices and burnt offerings, to placate His wrath and to win His favor, was the traditional form of worship for the pagan gods which the superstitious infancy of the human race had set up. But the higher conceptions upon which it was based purged it of the grosser rights of licentiousness that had prevailed in the personification of the productive powers of nature. The precepts and commands of Jehovah dealt with the material well-being of the subjects of His sovereignty. As the people advanced in enlightenment under their great leaders and teachers the sway of Jehovah was extended and exalted.

More and more the element of righteousness and justice assumed prominence, while that of loving-kindness and tender mercy began to assert itself. The God of Job and of the later Psalms is a different being from the God of the Pentateuch and the earlier annals. But the conception never reached a lofty height, compared to what is to be derived from modern knowledge and reason regarding the beneficent and all pervading Spirit of the universe. The early moral standards of the Jews, even when attributed directly to Jehovah, were not very high. Their conceptions of life never went beyond the earth, scarcely beyond that land in which they lived. Their religion was mainly patriotism; and their priestly and prophetic teachings were chiefly politics, with little of spirituality, though slowly the moral sense was lifted up and strengthened. They had no idea of immortality or of life after death, except that of a vague and shadowy continuance in the darkness of the underworld. Their precepts, their warnings, their promises and threats, derived as they believed, from their unseen Ruler, related only to their earthly welfare. Those whom they called prophets were concerned for their social and political condition as a people and their fate as a nation, more than for individual conduct and personal well-being.

Looking from the height of modern

intellectual and moral attainment, can we not see just how important to that which we were wont to call "modern civilization" was this Hebrew development of the idea of moral obligation, and of responsibility to a higher power, crude as it was? But was it so much more essential than the social and æsthetic development that sprang out of Hellas, or the conquering and organizing genius to which Rome gave birth? Were not even the Greek intelligence and the Roman power indispensable to the culture and dissemination of the Hebrew morality in the world? No bodily member is more essential than another;—all are requisite. Was the literature in which the Hebrew experience was embodied and preserved to after time more truly sacred or more inspired by the God of the universe than that which treasured up the other elements of human advancement toward perfection? It seemed so, because it related to moral duty and to the sentiments that controlled moral conduct and spirit ual growth; but, looking over the whole ground, was it?

We know now that this Holy Bible was a collection of writings gathered together at a late period in the Jewish history by priests and scribes from a mass of accumulated material. There was no attempt to make it consistent or harmonious. It contains the imperfections characteristic of the time, the people and the circumstances of its production.

There is a rude attempt to account for the origin of the world and its inhabitants, such as has been made by every distinct people on the earth, almost as soon as it has begun to keep written records. The Hebrew attempt, like the others, had the characteristics of an imperfect stage of intellectual development. It showed ignorance of material things and of natural phenomena and the superstition of a primitive time, for it was made before the light of science and philosophy had risen upon the world. Of course it cannot be reconciled with the knowledge of later ages.

Such an attempt to account for the origin of the earth and the human race, was a natural prelude to the annals of the nation. It was followed by a half-mythical account of the origin of the "chosen people," derived from the traditions of the Hebrew race, and then the annals gradually emerged from the legendary form into a clearer history. But they were made up by a mingling of traditions and conjectures with fragmentary and inconsistent records, and were generally crude in composition and arrangement, often conflicting and in many points incredible. And yet from the imperfect record man has been able to derive a knowledge, made constantly clearer by rational study, of the origin, early struggles, vigorous growth and ultimate decay of the nation from which some of our loftiest conceptions have been derived.

Mingled with these rude annals were stories of leaders and rulers, seers and prophets, of great men and of humble persons, from which valuable lessons were to be gained, as from other ancient tales of human experience. There too were found the regulations and commands of law-givers, the thoughts and speculations of wise men, the dreams and aspirations of poets, and the teachings, warnings and hopeful anticipations of those who have been called prophets, but whose prophesying was not so much a matter of prediction as of lofty political and personal morality, with threats and promises, attributed to Jehovah and dependent for fulfilment upon the conduct of the people.

This was a literature of an altogether human kind, offspring of the character, thought, feeling and experience of a people—an expression of the results of their life, preserved for the instruction of later generations of men. Therein it was like other literatures, but in its religious aspect it was superior to that of other ancient peoples in that it enshrined the experiences and teachings of a longer line of men of a higher moral and spiritual grade. The peculiar religious genius of the Hebrew race resulted in filling its erratic and imperfect literature with a larger proportion of permanent truth affecting the life and conduct of men than had been gained by others, and this gave it a powerful and lasting influence.

How petty are the long disputations of the devoutly learned upon the sacredness of Scripture, revelation of the divine will and inspirations of the authors of the old Hebrew writings. Is not God infinite spirit, pervading the universe with His presence and power and inspiring the whole movement of creation toward a perfect development which is still far from completed? Has not His inspiration wrought in all the processes of this development, in all worlds, in all races, in all history, in all literatures, tending to the one divine purpose of lifting the offspring of God into harmony with himself? Is not divine inspiration in every religion, to the extent that the people cherishing that religion have the capacity for giving expression to the divine that is in man?

To men on this earth the sources of revelation are the earth itself, the universe of which it is a part, and man's own nature and history. The meaning of these is truth, and man is left to find out truth with the aid of that within him which is divine. The more knowledge he acquires and the more accurately he reasons upon what he learns the nearer will he come to divine truth, and the greater will be his capacity for feeling the significance of this truth in relation to himself and to deity. The revelations of science and reason, and the intuitions of the philosophy which they inspire are more sacred than the dreams and oracles of seers and prophets who lived before the dawn of knowledge dispelled superstition.

The later times are the wiser, and have more of that inspiration which leads to the practical expression of truth than was possible in the old days, however deep may have been the insight into the human heart of some of the ancient teachers. Is it not folly to cling to old writings that are filled with the errors of ignorant and superstitious ages as peculiarly sacred scripture, or more the word of God than is the expression of the knowledge, thought and spiritual life of later times? In so far as they contain truth in harmony with ascertained facts in the realm of physical and human nature they may be held sacred; but in the same sense all writings that embody truth regarding the nature and destiny of man are sacred.

The study of all old literatures is instructive to mankind, and most of all that —whether Hebrew or heathen—which reveals the origin and development of the moral sense and of the religious instincts and aspirations. But man has wandered through a maze of darkness and error as the result of fixing his faith too exclusively upon a gathering of Books collected by the priests and scribes of an outgrown religion in a bygone age and pronounced "sacred" by the leaders of theological systems that have become antiquated. Yet he is even now emerging into the light where he can see that each generation must make its own scriptures and its own revelations. Holding fast that which is good in the revelations of the past, shall he not make the utmost use of the greater light that is shed upon his pathway and recognize its source as divine?

What is that doctrine of Evolution which so clearly explains the development of the material world and of physical life upon our planet but a new interpretation of the working of divine power? Has not that divine power wrought by an analogous process of progressive development toward symmetry and perfection through the intellectual and moral forces that operate in the spiritual nature of man? Was not the soul of man itself brought into being by evolution from the elements of sentient life through long generations of brute ancestry, and has it not been working toward its destiny of divine life under those orderly processes even until now? Is it not the all-pervading spirit of the universe that works in the human race toward the fulness of spiritual life in man, which was the object of creation?

In the stern old Hebrew race was developed the conception of purity in human life and of righteousness in human conduct, and with the inextinguishable torch of this high conception they struggled against the darkness of surrounding barbarism. If they imagined a terrible God, who promised them greatness and power as the reward of obedience to his commands and threatened dire calamities as the punishment of disobedience, it was through their faith in this mighty unseen Ruler that they kept alive the flame of that moral sense that was to elevate mankind from their primal stage of animalism, until a greater than the seers and prophets should arise to light a beacon with their torch. It was the great Jehovah and his worship, with all the awful sanctions with which it was surrounded, that kept the Hebrews up to their great task of inculcating righteousness and the submission of the brute in man to the divine.

After the long ferment of Judaism in the bosom of a single race, working out the sense of duty and of the relationship of man with the power that made him, while other qualities of the human soul were undergoing development in various parts of the world, there came the breaking over of the dividing lines and a coalescence of the forces of mental and moral evolution. Wherein is that span of human history from the scattering of the Hebrew nation to the appearance of the great Teacher of Galilee less sacred than that which preceded it, or the wide and varied literature in which the experience of humanity outside the Jewish race was then recorded less the embodiment of revelation for man than the Jewish Scriptures? In that long period, although the Hebrews were in a non-productive and spiritually apathetic state—their prophets dumb, their priests fanatical, their people crushed—yet both within and without their borders the forces were working which prepared the way for the next decisive process in the course of moral and spiritual evolution.

The development of a high moral sense and of lofty spiritual conceptions of man's relation and destiny was by no means confined to the Hebrew race, which found something to borrow from the Assyrian and Persian mythologies. It appeared in the teachings of the Chinese Confucius, and took an exalted form in the doctrines of the Hindoo Gautama. In no small degree it wrought upon Greek philosophy through Plato and Socrates, and was impressed upon the better part of Roman literature. The ferment was in the growing human race, and was part of the method of its moral and spiritual evolution. The soul of man was groping after a knowledge of its origin and its destiny. It was working out a revelation of both for its own benefit, and it contained within itself an inspiration that bore it ever upward.

The religious teachers of mankind in all times and all lands have been those who had the deepest insight into their nature and their relations in life, and the highest conceptions of their moral and spiritual needs, and of the means of satisfying them. Religious systems have ever been adapted to the needs of the time and the people for which they were established, and each was modified or displaced as the race advanced in power of thought and in moral strength and purity. They were the best means for spiritual elevation and moral advancement that the wisest and best men could devise for their own generation; but the time would always come when they hardened into forms that repressed growth instead of promoting it.

When once a system of faith and of worship had been fairly outgrown, one leader after another would struggle with the problem of replacing it with something adapted to a new era of progress, until at last the genius would appear who had greatness of soul enough to solve that problem for his fellow men and become their savior from the evils which tend to degradation.

Was not that wonderful teacher in Galilee such a genius? Did he not appear as the embodiment of a protest against the grosser and harsher phases of the old Jewish faith, its unspiritual conception of God as a stern ruler, and the ceremonies and observances through which His worship had become a dead formality, having no saving influence on the conduct of men? He was filled with an intense sympathy for the needs of humanity and had a profound insight that enabled him to bring to mankind a new gospel of salvation. Instead of being an unnatural (for that is what is meant by "supernatural") incarnation of divine power and wisdom, he was the incarnation of those human qualities which constitute moral perfection, the outworking of the divine which is incarnated in the imperfect human race. He had by natural endowment the ideal character toward which the human race was aspiring and striving, and toward which it must strive and aspire until perfection is reached. It was that which gave him his lofty conception of the deity as the Father of mankind instead of a terrible ruler; and of all men as brethren who had simply to establish the fraternal relation in their conduct toward each other in order to live in peace and happiness. It was that which raised him so immeasurably above all other teachers. It explains his comprehension of human needs, his intense sympathy and earnestness, and his power over those who came within his influence. It makes clear also the wonderful power which his personality has exercised in the world ever since he lived and died. Springing from a single branch of the human race, he had in perfection the noblest attributes of the race at large, and all men acknowledge his kinship.

Jesus of Nazareth was an embodiment

of the moral and religious genius of humanity, appearing at a time when the elements and process of human progress were prepared to receive a new impulse. His character was in a moral and spiritual sense the perfection of humanity, and it was divine in the sense that all humanity is divine in so far as it approaches its state of destined perfection. Of the secular interests of mankind in the world at large he knew little, and to them he gave little thought. Of the course of races and nations and the multifarious activities of life on its practical side he had little conception. In him the spiritual qualities of human nature found their highest and purest embodiment since the race began, and were most completely freed from the qualities that pertain to its physical origin and its physical needs. Hence his soul was in close sympathy with the spirit of divinity that pervades the universe and dwells in all life, and yielded itself absolutely to the impulse of divine love. By force of the marvellous endowments of his nature he was the teacher of those about him, and through them of all mankind. His mission, viewed in relation to its immediate scope and effect, was humble, almost insignificant, and the history of the time scarce took notice of it. But in such a life and character, and the teachings that accompanied them, there was something inextinguishable. There was a light kindled that could not fail to spread for the illumination of the world.

It is no wonder that such a phenomenon at such a time and place should come to be regarded as miraculous, as soon as people got far enough from it to discern its true proportions. It is not strange that in a record made up a century or more after the marvellous appearance, in a time and among a people of little accuracy in knowledge and reasoning, tales of a supernatural origin, of supernatural powers and of miraculous accompaniments of the birth, life and death of such a being should be devoutly accepted.

A perfect man at that time, devoted to an effort to make all mankind perfect! And especially a man who bore his glad tidings to those who were at that time universally despised and down-trodden— the poor! What could be more wonderful and more calculated to excite superstitious faith in his divinity, in an age when divinity was attributed to all manner of exceptional persons?

It is not strange if those who founded a new religious system upon his teachings connected his appearance and mission with the long-cherished Messianic hopes of Israel, and gave their fulfilment a spiritual turn. It is not to be wondered at if they saw in him the embodiment of the vague foreshadowings of seers and prophets, and tried to make the dimly remembered and imperfectly recorded facts of his life and teachings conform to the prophesies of the old Jewish Scriptures. Yet no man ever appeared on the earth more completely unheralded.

As our vision becomes broader and

clearer, we are more and more believers in the large designs of the Almighty and the Providence that works in the laws of the universe, and nothing is plainer than the preparation of the soil of the human race for the seed sown by the teacher of Nazareth. Hebrew history, with its theocratic idea of moral human government, Grecian history, with its development of sentiment and refinement and intellectuality, and Roman history, with the growth of the elements of conquest and power for reducing to order and system,—these were the chief factors that made the world ready for the gospel of purity and unselfish goodness. That gospel was the mighty leaven needed for the seething mass of humanity; but ages were required for the fermentation, and it is far from finished now. When the whole lump is leavened, then will the Kingdom of God have come upon the earth.

But why should we overlook or try to explain away the imperfections and inconsistences of the human record in which the incidents of the life and teachings of Jesus have been preserved? Why not rather admit that it is a purely human record, and try to separate from the errors which it contains the pure truth which is alone of enduring value? That later Scripture, long held sacred, is so only according to the measure of truth which it contains for the elevation of mankind, and it is to be judged like other literature, according to the rules of reason and with reference to the circumstances of its production. The incredible is not to be believed. That which is not according to nature is not to be accepted. Out of the blending of legends and dim traditions, the tales of credulity and superstition, the conflicting statements of hearsay evidence, and the writings of those who sought to support their doctrines and theories by events which occurred before these were formed, we should seek to extract the simplicity of truth.

In the remarkable episode in human development which had its impulse in the soul of a Galilean peasant, there is no doubt a revelation to Man; but it is a revelation derived from his own experience, which has been in manifold ways misinterpreted. Out of a character of divine purity and strength, out of teachings of divine simplicity and force, because in the highest sense human, superstition wrought forms of faith and worship adapted to the transient needs of mankind. Human minds, with defective knowledge and perverted spiritual sense, striving with problems beyond their compass and dealing with men in whose souls superstition and hereditary passion held sway, devised creeds and set up forms of worship that served for restraint and for elevation in their day. All systems of belief are made and modified by man to suit the needs of his spiritual growth, and they have a divine sanction just so far as man has found out truth and given it embodiment.

Forms of belief have changed with the progress of the race and must change or die. But through the mass of human error and imperfection has wrought for centuries the leaven of the imperishable gospel of purity and unselfishness. With increasing knowledge and with strengthening reason ancient dogmas shrivel into dust, but only to reveal the truth more clearly. The million wrongs and evils with which humanity struggles in its upward course are due to the selfish instincts which were elements of strength to the race in fighting its way from its brute origin, conquering the conditions of growth and battling for the mastery of the world. But these selfish instincts derived from an ancestry of brutes, and necessary in early stages of struggle, are at war with the spiritual instincts. All come from the inspiration of divinity; but perfectness will not be gained till the spirit overcomes the flesh. In the strife of these forces is the battle of life for man.

The latest revelations are the revelations of reason, wrought out of the knowledge which science and history afford. They are as sacred to-day as were ever the oracles of the olden time, and they render obsolete every belief with which they are inconsistent. But nothing in man's knowledge or reason can impair the efficacy of the gospel of purity and self-sacrifice. In the subjugation of selfish instincts and the devotion of effort to the good of others lies the salvation of the individual and of the race. That is a doctrine which no science or philosophy can transcend ; and no progress in knowledge or in reasoning can dim the lustre of the character of the Teacher of Nazareth or supersede the everlasting truth of his most essential precepts so far as they bear upon human conduct ; indeed, rightly read, they confirm the fundamental verity of his principles. Truths cannot be inconsistent with each other.

No wonder if in a superstitious age he was exalted to divinity and has been long held representative of God to man. But he was a man of men, the type of what man may be on the moral and spiritual side, and it is that which makes of him an enduring example. The pre-eminently human teacher who sprang out of the bosom of decaying Judaism to give new moral and spiritual light to the world has for ages been petrified by superstition, incrusted with dogmas and swathed in theological subtleties. Unto some he has become an imposing idol containing the mysterious person of unseen divinity, and has been enshrined in temples as a God, while to others he has been made as a mummy, worshipped but not followed, holding no vital relation with the living human race.

It is the mission of modern knowledge and untrammelled reason, in exploring the realm of physical science and sounding the depths of human philosophy, in subjecting past history and literature to the test of unflinching criticism, to extract the revelation of truth from whatever is; and they should restore to humanity its greatest Teacher, by restoring humanity to him. All revelation of man's destiny is made by man to man; and all his search is to find out God.

THE END.

"*A brainy little volume.*"—Providence Telegram.

MIDNIGHT TALKS
At the Club.

Reported by AMOS K. FISKE.

Contents: The "*Owl Party;*" Temperance; The Shepherdless Sheep; Sunday Observance; Religion; Political Immorality; Superstition and Worship; The Scriptures as a Fetich; Irish-Americans; Moses and the Prophets; Ancient Scriptures; Value of Human Evidence; Power of Personality; Discussions Applied; Usefulness of Delusion; The Faith Defended; Toleration and Enlightenment; Comfort in Essential Truths.

"A delightful book. . . . Covering a multitude of subjects with a kindly light of wit and wisdom."—Jno. Boyle O'Reilly, Boston.

"The opinions are those of a broad-minded, earnest man of to-day, an optimist of the better sort, and they are written in crisp and cogent style."—*Providence Journal.*

"The 'Owl Party' of four who do most of the talking, are a bright and brainy quartette."—*Buffalo Express.*

"Full of suggestion to the thoughtful."—*San Francisco Chronicle.*

"Healthful, with humor and seriousness most happily blended for the making of a book that is at once pleasant and wise."—*Evening Bulletin, Philadelphia.*

"Oftentimes eloquent and at all times sincere, even when the playful humor lies beaming on the surface, it is a book that will carry light and consolation to many doubting minds."—*New York Times.*

"Although the subjects are not new, yet there is a freshness about their treatment which gives an impression of novelty, and one feels the inspiration of a certain breadth and liberality of thought which is uncommon in discussions of this sort."—*Boston Post.*

"This candor of mind, and a certain sweetness of temper are very alluring to the reader, who, whether he finds his own pet beliefs confirmed or gently taken apart, and their incongruities made clear, will enjoy every step of the process."—*Brooklyn Times.*

"Read with pleasure and laid aside with regret when the last page is reached."—*Boston Saturday Evening Gazette.*

"Keen insight, clear discernment, strong convictions, and distinct individuality of thought. . . . Attractive to those who wish to be nourished through their intelligence rather than through their prejudices."—*The Christian Union, N. Y.*

16mo, Vellum Cloth, gilt top, $1.00.

FORDS, HOWARD, & HULBERT,
30 *Lafayette Place, New York.*

Works of Biography

PUBLISHED BY

FORDS, HOWARD, & HULBERT,

30 *Lafayette Place, New York.*

Sir Philip Sidney: His Life and Times. By Mrs. S. M. HENRY DAVIS, Author of "Norway Nights and Russian Days." *Steel portrait* of Sidney. 12mo. New popular edition. Cloth, $1.25.

"Compels the reader's attention, and leaves upon his mind impressions more distinct and lasting than the greatest historians are in the habit of making. . . . We long to see the story of Sidney's life take its proper place in the hearts of American youth."—*Christian Union.*

Abraham Lincoln: The True Story of a Great Life. By WM. OSBORNE STODDARD, Secretary to President Lincoln. 8vo. Cloth, *illustrated*, $2.00.

"Graphic and entertaining . . . as rich in incident as any romance, and sparkling with wise wit and racy anecdote. It comprises a large mass of valuable and judiciously epitomized information."—*Harper's Monthly.*

Henry Ward Beecher: His Personality, Career and Influence in Public Affairs. By JOHN R. HOWARD. *With portraits.* 8vo., 164 pp. Cloth, 75 cents.

"Altogether the finest bit of biographic work that has been done in many a day."—ALBION W. TOURGEE.

"Gives a well-proportioned view of Beecher's whole career, and is enriched with many personal reminiscences, anecdotes and letters accumulated by Mr. Howard during his forty years of intimate friendship and twenty of close association in literary and business matters with Mr. Beecher, as his publisher."—*Brooklyn Times.*

Bismarck: His Authentic Biography. By GEORGE HEZEKIEL. *Historical Introduction* by BAYARD TAYLOR. *Profusely Illustrated: New Map, etc.* 8vo. Half morocco, $4.

"Noteworthy for the fullness of its details and the great variety of hitherto unknown facts and incidents that are recorded in it."—*N. Y. Sun.*

Bryant and His Friends: A Memoir of Wm. Cullen Bryant, and Reminiscences of the best-known Knickerbocker Writers—Irving, Halleck, Paulding, Cooper, Dana, etc., etc. By JAMES GRANT WILSON *Illustrated* with portraits and manuscript fac-similes. Cloth, beveled, gilt top, $2.00.

"A standard volume of literary history."—*Boston Traveller.*

Life and Letters of John H. Raymond. Organizer and First President of Vassar College. Edited by HARRIET RAYMOND LLOYD. 8vo. *Steel Portrait.* Ex. cloth, beveled, $2.50.

"A book, the charm of which it is not easy to express. . . . This admirably judicious record of a wholly and singularly beautiful, strong, wise, consecrated life."—*Chicago Advance.*

Choice Works of Fiction,

PUBLISHED BY

FORDS, HOWARD, & HULBERT,

30 *Lafayette Place, New York.*

ANONYMOUS. **A Palace-Prison**; or, the Past and the Present. Sanity Amid the Insane. $1.00.

HENRY WARD BEECHER. **Norwood**: a Tale of Village Life in New England. $1.25.

ALEXANDRE BIDA. **Aucassin and Nicolette**: The Lovers of Provence. Song-Story, from French of XIIth Century, trans by A. R. MACDONOUGH. *Illustrated by* BIDA. $1.50.

HELEN CAMPBELL. **Under Green Apple Boughs.** *Illustrated.* $1.00.

JULIUS CHAMBERS. **On a Margin.** A Novel of Wall Street and Washington. $1.25.

CHAS. M. CLAY. **The Modern Hagar.** Southern View of the War. $1.50.

ALICE C. HALL. **Miss Leighton's Perplexities.** A Love Story. $1.00.

WM. J. HARSHA. **Ploughed Under:** The Story of an Indian Chief. $1.00.

JULIAN HAWTHORNE. **Dust.** A Novel. *With Portrait and Illustrations.* $1.25.

NATHAN C. KOUNS. **Dorcas:** A Tale of the Catacombs. *Illustrated by* WILL LOW. $1.25.

ORPHEUS C. KERR (R. H. NEWELL). **There Was Once a Man.** (Inverted Darwinism.) *Illustrated.* $1.50.

MRS. A. G. PADDOCK. **The Fate of Madame La Tour.** Mormonism in Utah. $1.00.

BLANCHE ROOSEVELT. **Stage-Struck:** or, She Would be an Opera Singer. $1.50.

ALBION W. TOURGEE. **Murvale Eastman:** Christian Socialist; Hot Plowshares; A Royal Gentleman; Figs and Thistles; A Fool's Errand; Bricks Without Straw. *Illustrated.* $1.50 per vol. John Eax, and other Stories; Black Ice. $1.25 per vol.

WM. A. WILKINS. **The Cleverdale Mystery:** The Political Machine and its Wheels. Paper, 40 cents.

GEO. F. WILLIAMS. **Bullet and Shell:** A Story of War as the Soldier Saw it. *Illustrated* by Edwin Forbes. Popular edition. 8vo., cloth, $2.00.

Two Notable Novels.

MURVALE EASTMAN:
Christian Socialist.

By Albion W. Tourgee.

This is one of Tourgee's most vivid works, dealing with the great problems of the day as to labor, capital, poverty, wealth, journalism, speculation, etc., but through the medium of a tale of peculiar power. *Cloth, decorated,* $1.50.

"You have written a great book in *Murvale Eastman.* It should be read as widely as *A Fool's Errand,* for it is a better, stronger, riper book. It is vastly superior to *Looking Backward,* since it makes every reader look Christ-ward. . . . I wish every minister, every working man, every millionaire and every political economist would read it."—Bishop John H. Vincent.

"I have read it with intense interest."—U. S. Senator Wm. P. Frye.

"It should be read by everyone who is not fully satisfied with things as they are. It would be fortunate if this book were read by thousands upon thousands."—Hugh O. Pentecost.

"Full of the striking picturesqueness of romantic scenes, artistically selected and vividly portrayed."—*Boston Traveller.*

"Judge Tourgee has struck many valiant and trenchant blows in the cause of the oppressed, but even his *Fool's Errand* will not equal in strength, scope and thrilling interest as a story this powerfully elucidated illustration of the Christ-given principle of socialism."—*Boston Home Journal.*

"Summed up, this novel needs a twofold classification. It is a rattling broadside against the unscrupulous, and a highly dramatic story."—*New York Sun.*

JUGGERNAUT:
A Veiled Record.

By Geo. Cary Eggleston and Dolores Marbourg.

A masterly depiction of the perils of ambition for the getting of wealth and power in American life. Cloth, with design by Ipsen, $1.25.

"No tangle of plot, but a keen and irresistible story of two lives; swift, straight, and brilliant as a sword-thrust—and as terrible."—Howard's Column in *New York Press.*

"The story will be read for its tragic pathos. The moral needs no emphasis."—*Christian Union.*

"A story of remarkable power."—*Christian at Work.*

*** *Sold by all Booksellers, or mailed, on receipt of the price, by*
FORDS, HOWARD, & HULBERT,
30 Lafayette Place, New York.

A Great Work Completed.

THE LIFE OF JESUS, THE CHRIST.

By Henry Ward Beecher.

Completed Edition. Vol. I entire, and Vol. II to end of Chapter XXV, stand as Mr. Beecher finished them. Chapters XXVI to XXXII, concluding the second volume, have been carefully compiled from the Author's Sermons along the line of the topics involved, by his son, Wm. C. Beecher and Rev. Samuel Scoville.

Issued in two vols., 8vo; richly illustrated with steel and wood engravings and three Maps. Cloth, $5.50; library style, $7.50; half morocco, $9.50. Volumes separately, for those who wish to complete old sets: Cloth, $3.00; library style, $4.00; half morocco, $5.00. (Parties who have Vol. II in good condition and would like to have the two volumes in new and identical binding, are invited to correspond with the undersigned.)

Fragments of Opinion when Vol. I was issued.

"The ordinary overflowing exuberance of his style, its manifold illustrations, its boldness and occasional homeliness, its perpetual play of wit and sarcasm, are here abated; the marvelous majesty and beauty of the person of Jesus have had an elevating and chastening power. The result is a dignity almost uniformly sustained, and now and then passages of exquisite beauty."—*Presbyterian Quarterly and Princeton Review.*

"The great poet-preacher of our day has prepared for the Church a marvelous gallery of pictures. . . . No one can easily lay aside the book when once he commences its perusal until he has completed the last page; and all will anxiously await the publication of the concluding volume."—*Christian Advocate, New York.*

"In the best qualities of historical composition, in bold grouping, strong delineation, clear narrative, the book is all that could be asked for; and the constant recurrence of metaphors and illustrations from the natural world has a singular appropriateness and beauty in the story of one who so constantly taught by like methods."—*Boston Daily Advertiser, Mass.*

"We perpetually feel the author's master-power as he darts forth a condensed argument in a single illustration. This quality makes the work eminently suggestive, and every minister, teacher, parent and thinking person will find it of great consequence to keep by him for frequent reference and use."—*New York Standard.*

⁎ *Sold by all Booksellers, or mailed, on receipt of the price, by*

FORDS, HOWARD, & HULBERT,

30 Lafayette Place, New York.

An Ample Record.

A Biography of Rev. Henry Ward Beecher.

BY WM. C. BEECHER AND REV. SAMUEL SCOVILLE, ASSISTED BY MRS. HENRY WARD BEECHER.

This standard work, known generally as "The Family Biography," to distinguish it from the many hasty and ephemeral compilations sold as giving the "life" of Mr. Beecher, has intrinsic merits which are more and more recognized as it takes its permanent place. It gives ample details of Mr. Beecher's childhood, youth and early manhood; copious extracts from his characteristic diaries, and graphic portrayals of his experiences and conflicts as a preacher of Christ and a champion of liberty. Every page possesses a fascination growing out of the subject. The tribulations and sorrows of the great preacher are not passed over lightly, as many advised, but are calmly and sorrowfully set forth in clear perspective, as befits an impartial history.

One vol., large 8vo, 713 pp. With fine steel engraving of H. W. Beecher, and copious index. Cloth, $3.00; sheep, $3.50; red seal, $3.75; half morocco, $4.50; full morocco, $6.

"Will always be the best personal biography of Mr. Beecher—the one which contains the most of his own personality. . . . The editors have wisely kept themselves in the background, and making use of the autobiographical material which Mr. Beecher left in the form of letters and in personal reminiscences scattered through his writings, they have woven together a narrative of which Mr. Beecher may be truly said to be himself the author."—*Christian Union.*

"Every word in this book has been read by us with the deepest interest. . . . A narrative in which truthfulness is patent in every line. . . . We heartily commend the reading of this book to those who desire to obtain an inside as well as an outside view of Mr. Beecher's life."—*Pulpit Treasury, N. Y.*

"Rich in its collection of facts, it bears evidence of singular industry and devotion on the part of its compilers. . . . On the whole the book is one of remarkable interest, and will, we think, grow in public favor."—*North American Review.*

⁎⁎⁎ Sold by all Booksellers, or mailed, on receipt of the price, by

FORDS, HOWARD, & HULBERT,

30 Lafayette Place, New York.

SOUTHERN CALIFORNIA.

Says
CHARLES DUDLEY WARNER:

"Mr. THEODORE S. VAN DYKE, a graduate of a New England college, has lived nearly twenty years in Southern California, and hunted, fished and tramped over every acre of it. He is the most competent, accomplished, and level-headed historian California ever had. He has a very practical turn, and is thoroughly up in agriculture, horticulture, the problem of immigration, etc. Besides all this, he has uncommon powers of description and a genuine literary gift. It is not claiming too much to say that he is on the Pacific coast what John Burroughs is on the Atlantic. But he has more humor than Burroughs, and an equally keen instinct of nature. His former book on 'Southern California' is altogether the best that has been written, and it is so because Mr Van Dyke has the literary art, which is the art of seeing things as they are."

Southern California: Its Valleys, Hills and Streams; its Animals, Birds and Fishes; its Gardens, Farms and Climate. 12mo. Ex. cloth, beveled. $1.50.

"Reading it makes one long at once to be away to taste the delights of that charming country."—*London* (Eng.) *Graphic.*

The Still Hunter: A Popular Treatise on Deer Stalking. 12mo. Ex. cloth, beveled. $2.00.

"The best, the very best work on deer hunting."—*Spirit of the Times.*
"Altogether the best and most complete American book we have yet seen on any branch of field sports."—*New York Evening Post.*

Millionaires of a Day: An Inside History of the Great Southern California Boom. 12mo. Ex. cloth, $1; paper, 50 cents.

"A witty and entertaining, but withal valuable and shrewd description of real and fanciful growth of a most favored land."—*Detroit Tribune.*

Rifle, Rod and Gun in California: A Sporting Romance. 12mo. Ex. cloth, beveled, $1.50.

"Crisp and readable throughout, and, at the same time, gives a full and truthful technical account of our Southern California game, afoot, afloat, or on the wing."—*San Francisco Alta California.*

FORDS, HOWARD, & HULBERT,
30 Lafayette Place, New York.

www.ingramcontent.com/pod-product-compliance
Lightning Source LLC
Chambersburg PA
CBHW021810230426
43669CB00008B/706